GUIDE-BOOK

OF THE

LEHIGH VALLEY RAILROAD

AND

ITS SEVERAL BRANCHES AND CONNECTIONS;

WITH AN ACCOUNT, DESCRIPTIVE AND HISTORICAL,

OF THE

PLACES ALONG THEIR ROUTE;

INCLUDING ALSO

A HISTORY OF THE COMPANY FROM ITS FIRST ORGANIZATION, AND INTERESTING FACTS CONCERNING THE ORIGIN AND GROWTH OF THE COAL AND IRON TRADE IN THE LEHIGH AND WYOMING REGIONS.

HANDSOMELY ILLUSTRATED FROM RECENT SKETCHES.

PREFIXED TO WHICH IS A MAP OF THE ROAD AND ITS CONNECTIONS.

PHILADELPHIA:
J. B. LIPPINCOTT & CO.
1873.

OFFICERS

OF THE

LEHIGH VALLEY RAILROAD COMPANY,

JANUARY 21st, 1873.

President,
ASA PACKER,
MAUCH CHUNK.

Vice-President,
CHARLES HARTSHORNE,
PHILADELPHIA.

Treasurer,
LLOYD CHAMBERLAIN,
PHILADELPHIA.

Secretary,
JOHN R. FANSHAWE,
PHILADELPHIA.

General Superintendent and Chief Engineer,
ROBERT H. SAYRE,
BETHLEHEM.

DIRECTORS.

CHARLES HARTSHORNE,
WILLIAM W. LONGSTRETH,
J. GILLINGHAM FELL,
JOHN TAYLOR JOHNSTON,
WILLIAM H. GATZMER,
DAVID THOMAS,
ASHBEL WELCH,
ARIO PARDEE,
WILLIAM L. CONYNGHAM,
WILLIAM A. INGHAM,
JOSEPH WHARTON,
GEORGE B. MARKLE.

President's Assist. and Gen. Agt.,	WM. H. SAYRE, *Bethlehem.*
Assistant General Superintendent,	H. STANLEY GOODWIN, *Bethlehem.*
Supt. Beaver Meadow Division,	A. G. BRODHEAD, *Mauch Chunk.*
" *Mahanoy* "	JAS. I. BLAKSLEE, *Mauch Chunk.*
" *Wyoming* "	A. MITCHELL, *Wilkes-Barre.*
General Freight Agent,	JOHN TAYLOR, *Mauch Chunk.*
Cashier,	WM. C. MORRIS, JR., *Mauch Chunk.*
Purchasing Agent,	L. CHAMBERLAIN, *Philadelphia.*
Master Mechanics,	JOHN I. KINSEY, *Easton.* DAVID CLARK, *Hazleton.* JOHN CAMPBELL, *Delano.* PHILIP HOFECKER, *Weatherly.*

OFFICERS

OF THE

PENNSYLVANIA AND NEW YORK CANAL AND RAILROAD COMPANY.

President.
ROBERT H. SAYRE.

Treasurer.
CHARLES HARTSHORNE.

General Superintendent.
ROBERT A. PACKER.

Directors.

Asa Packer,
Wm. W. Longstreth,
Chas. Hartshorne,
Robert A. Packer,
Victor E. Piollet,
Garrett B. Linderman,
J. Henry Swoyer,
John J. Taylor,
Robert Lockhart,
Jno. W. Hollenback,
Wm. H. Sayre,
Joseph Wharton.

PREFACE.

THIS Guide-Book has been prepared with great care and fidelity, as well from past historical documents as from recent and reliable information. In doing so, the writer has freely availed himself of the aid given by other publications, while very much of the matter is wholly original, and has been obtained directly from the places and establishments described. He desires to acknowledge gratefully his obligations to the officials of the Company and other residents along its road for the valuable help so kindly rendered him. He would be still further thankful if those readers who may discover errors in what is here printed will inform him of the same. Such communications may be addressed to the President's Assistant at Bethlehem.

L. C.

June 1st, 1873.

HISTORY

OF THE

LEHIGH VALLEY RAILROAD CO

FROM ITS ORGANIZATION TO THE PRESENT DATE.

As preliminary to an account of the different towns on the route of the Lehigh Valley Railroad and its various branches, it may be interesting to give a brief sketch of its history.

This railroad was originally incorporated under the name of the Delaware, Lehigh, Schuylkill and Susquehanna Railroad Company, by an Act of Assembly passed April 21st, 1846. The bill was prepared at the suggestion and through the agency of a few enterprising and far-seeing citizens of Northampton and Lehigh Counties. There was strong opposition to it, and it was carried through the Legislature mainly by the exertions of Dr. Jesse Samuel, a Representative from Lehigh County. There seemed to be but little faith in the project on the part of capitalists; for, although the commissioners named in the act promptly advertised for subscriptions to the stock, it was not until the 2d of August, 1847, that a sufficient amount for a commencement could be secured. On that day 5002 shares had been taken, on each of which an installment of five dollars had been paid. After considerable trouble, the letters patent were issued, and on the 21st day of October, 1847, the first election for officers was held, resulting as follows: President, James M. Porter; Managers, Dudley S. Gregory, John S. Dorsey, John P. Jackson, Daniel McIntyre, Edward R. Biddle, and John N. Hutchinson; Secretary, John N. Hutchinson. These officers were re-elected for the years 1847, 1848, 1849, and 1850. In the months of October, November, and December, 1850, the first survey of the road was made, from the mouth of the Mahoning Creek to Easton, by Roswell B. Mason, civil engineer. Early in 1851 the Canal Commissioners of the State appointed Jacob Dillinger and Jesse Samuel, engineers, to examine whether the proposed railroad would not injure the canal of the Lehigh Coal and Navigation Company or obstruct its works. They reported that it would not, and the Board immediately authorized Mr. Hutchinson to commence the construction of the railroad, the time limited by the charter for its beginning having almost expired. Mr. Dillinger was appointed Superintendent, and Dr. Samuel, Engineer, and under their supervision the work was prosecuted, and during the spring and summer about one mile was graded immediately below Allentown. The landholders on that part of the route released all claims for damages for a nominal consideration.

On the 31st of October, 1851, Asa Packer became the purchaser of nearly all the stock which had been subscribed, and commenced to obtain additional subscriptions, with a view to the prompt construction of the road.

In the spring of 1852, Mr. Robert H. Sayre, at that time holding a responsible situation with the Lehigh Coal and Navigation Company, was appointed Chief Engineer of the railroad company, and on the 11th of May commenced the survey and location of the line, completing it in the latter part of June. About the 1st of October he again engaged a corps, and started upon the permanent location of the road, finishing it during the fall and winter.

On the 27th of November, 1852, Judge Packer submitted a proposition (which was duly accepted) for constructing the railroad from opposite Mauch Chunk, where it would intersect the Beaver Meadow Railroad, to Easton, where it would connect with the New Jersey Central Railroad and the Belvidere Delaware Railroad, and thus furnish outlets for its trade to the two great cities, New York and Philadelphia. Judge Packer agreed to receive as payment for this work the company's stock and bonds, and work was commenced immediately at Mauch Chunk and Easton.

On the 7th of January, 1853, the name of the Company was changed by Act of Assembly to that of the Lehigh Valley Railroad Company, and on the 10th of that month James M. Porter was re-elected President; John N. Hutchinson, Treasurer and Secretary; William Hackett, David Barnet, William H. Gatzmer, Henry King, John T. Johnston, and John O. Stearns, Managers.

Judge Packer prosecuted the work with unceasing vigor, notwithstanding the formidable obstructions encountered in making the roadway at different points through the rocky bluffs, in some places rising to great height. He had the work at Rockdale (the particulars of which will be found under that head) and at some other difficult points done by the day. At Easton also the road was constructed at heavy expense through a solid and extensive bed of limestone.

During the summer of 1853, the advance in the prices of labor, materials, provisions, etc., and the unusual amount of sickness then prevailing along the whole line (it was at this time that cholera visited this region), retarded the work very greatly.

A subsequent contract for connection with the Belvidere Delaware Railroad at Phillipsburg without ascending grade involved an entire change of plan, much delay, and a consequent increase in the cost of bridge and adjoining improvements. The task imposed was to connect with two roads on the east bank of the Delaware River, running at right angles to each other, and varying about twenty-two feet in elevation. This required a style of bridge as yet wholly unknown, the successful building of which was a theme of general interest and congratulation. Much of the difficulty also attending its construction arose from the frequent and continued high water. To obviate this trouble, the greater part of the structure was raised upon wire cables stretched from pier to pier,—a novel undertaking, which was satisfactorily accomplished.

In this early period of the history of the road, valued aid was rendered by several gentlemen connected with the Central Railroad of New Jersey in the purchase of its stocks and bonds, and by the Camden and Amboy Railroad Company, which loaned its securities to the contractor; the community at large not having as yet enough faith in the success of this new enterprise to make its own securities sufficiently available.

The road was opened for the transportation of passengers from South Easton to Allentown, June 11th, 1855, and two trains ran daily to the latter place until September 12th, when the road was opened for travel to Mauch Chunk,—one train a day being run until the 1st of October. Up to this time, the road was operated by Judge Packer with rolling stock hired from the Central Railroad Company of New Jersey. The road was accepted from the contractor from and after September 24th. Up to the 19th of November, the Central Railroad Company ran two passenger trains daily from Easton to Mauch Chunk, connecting with the Philadelphia trains on the Belvidere Delaware Railroad. At this date one of the passenger trains was withdrawn, a freight train with passenger car being substituted. This arrangement proving unsatisfactory, and a passenger locomotive and four cars having been in the mean time purchased, on the 24th of December the passenger train connecting with the early and late trains from New York and Philadelphia was run by the Lehigh Valley Railroad Company, the Central Company still running the mid-day train. At the same time, a daily freight train was put upon the road, leaving Easton in the morning and returning in the evening.

The receipts from passengers during these three months were larger than was anticipated. Those from coal and miscellaneous freight were limited by want of cars. The coal, iron, and ore were transported in cars furnished by the Central Railroad Company, the Beaver Meadow Railroad and Coal Company, and

Packer, Carter & Co. In the early part of October, an arrangement was made with Howard & Co., of Philadelphia, to do the freighting business of the road (except coal, iron, and iron ore), they furnishing cars, train-hands, etc., and paying a fixed rate per mile for toll and transportation. An arrangement was also effected with the Hope Express Company, of New York, for carrying the express-matter at a given sum per month.

The receipts and expenditures were as follows:

RECEIPTS.

	Coal.	Passengers.	Freight.	Total.
October	$912 47	$6,812.93	$94.34	$7,819.74
November	2,648.42	6,223.44	590.03	9,461.89
December	1,792.43	5,675.44	1,768.45	9,236.32
				$26,517.95

EXPENSES.

October	$4,501.15	
November	5,350.60	
December	13,884.58	
		23,736.33
Net profit		$2,781.62

In the beginning of the year 1856, it was thought necessary to remove the main office of the Company to Philadelphia. Judge Porter on this account declined a re-election to the presidency, and, on February 5th, Mr. Wm. W. Longstreth was chosen to fill the vacancy, but resigned on the 13th of May following, when Mr. J. Gillingham Fell was elected President.

In the year 1857, the North Pennsylvania Railroad was completed to Bethlehem, and immediate connection was thus obtained with Philadelphia by the Lehigh Valley Railroad.

During the year 1857, the Catasauqua and Fogelsville Railroad (designed for the supply of iron ore to the various furnaces along the Lehigh) was completed, connecting with the Lehigh Valley Railroad at Catasauqua.

In 1858, connection was formed between the Quakake Railroad (now the Mahanoy Division) and the Catawissa Railroad for Catawissa, Rupert, Danville, Williamsport, Elmira, etc.

During the year 1859, the East Pennsylvania Road was finished and put into operation, thus forming a valuable junction with the connections between New York and the West, to complete which seventeen miles of the Lehigh Valley Road are used. During the same year the Lehigh Luzerne Railroad, connecting the Hazleton Road with the Black Creek Valley, was finished, by which another large and valuable field of coal was opened to the market.

During the year 1860, the large shops at Easton, for the manufacture and repair of engines and cars, were built. In January, 1862, steel fire-boxes were first used. In June of this year the disastrous freshet, alluded to more fully under the head of White aven, occurred, causing great damage to the road, and for awhile seriously impairing its business. In this same year Mr. Fell resigned the presidency of the Company, and Judge Packer was elected in his stead.

In 1863, steel tires were first introduced. During this same year forty-seven acres of land were bought at Burlington (now Packerton), for the more convenient making-up of coal trains, and for the erection of car-

and machine-shops, which were put at once under construction.

In 1864, Judge Packer resigned the presidency of the road, and Mr. Wm. W. Longstreth was elected to fill the vacancy.

On the 8th of July, 1864, by the unanimous approval of the stockholders of the respective companies, this Company incorporated with itself the Beaver Meadow Railroad and the Penn Haven and White Haven Railroad. The former road, with double track, extended from East Mauch Chunk to Penn Haven, and from thence to Beaver Meadow, and by its various branches to the adjoining mines in Carbon and Schuylkill Counties. By this union the Lehigh Valley Railroad Company became owners also of a considerable body of coal land near the village of Beaver Meadow. The second of the two roads thus merged extended from Penn Haven Junction to White Haven, a distance of seventeen miles. By the acquisition of these several roads, and by their various important connections, the Lehigh Valley Railroad added at once very largely to its business of every description, and was put in a position of still greater prosperity for the immediate future. At the same time, by its subscription to the stock of the Lehigh and Mahanoy Railroad Company, it was aiding materially a near extension of its business in other important directions.

During the year 1865 the second track between Easton and Mauch Chunk was laid. During this same year the Lehigh Coal and Navigation Company announced their determination to build from Penn Haven to White Haven. This made it necessary, in order to secure a portion of the Wilkes-Barre trade, to put the extension of the Lehigh Valley Railroad under contract, which was promptly done. About this time also the Morris and Essex Railroad was opened, connecting with the Lehigh Valley at Phillipsburg, and reaching to Hoboken, giving increased facility to trade in that direction.

In June, 1866, by the unanimous action of both companies, the Lehigh and Mahanoy Railroad was merged with the Lehigh Valley Railroad, thus adding $2,145,850 to the capital of this latter company, and greatly increasing its capacities and facilities. The length of the main line thus added, from Black Creek to Mount Carmel, is forty miles, of sidings and short branches twenty and three-quarter miles more. In the early part of this same year, Judge Packer purchased, on behalf of the Lehigh Valley Railroad Company, a controlling interest in the North Branch Canal, extending from Wilkes-Barre to the New York State line, a distance of over one hundred miles, with a charter from the Commonwealth authorizing the Company to change its corporate title to the Pennsylvania and New York Canal and Railroad Company, and to build a railroad the entire length. The canal was valued in this arrangement at $1,050,000, over three-fourths of which are embraced in the purchase.

During this same year, subscriptions were received for 24,462 additional shares of stock, amounting to $1,323,100, for the purpose of extending the railroad from White Haven to the Wyoming Valley.

On May 29th, 1867, the extension of the road to Wilkes-Barre was opened for business, amid the hearty congratulations of all the residents of the Wyoming

Valley. The construction of the road thence to Waverly was prosecuted vigorously, portions from Wilkes-Barre to Pittston, and from Towanda to the State line, having been brought into active and profitable use.

On June 1st, 1868, by a merger of the stock of the Hazleton Railroad Company, and soon thereafter by a similar merger of the Lehigh Luzerne Railroad Company, the Lehigh Valley Railroad Company came into possession of said roads, rights, franchises, and property. By these two mergers, and by purchase of rolling stock and other property from the lessees, there inured to this Company a total length of tracks of sixty-five miles, also about eighteen hundred acres of valuable coal lands, a large amount of town lots and other real estate, cars, machinery, etc.

In August, this Company purchased the railroad of the Spring Mountain Coal Company from Leviston to Jeanesville, and about October 1st grading was commenced for a short extension towards Yorktown and towards the mines of the German Pennsylvania Coal Company. On November 2d the road of the P. & N. Y. C. & R. R. Co. was opened for business from the Lackawanna and Bloomsburg Junction to Tunkhannock. In June, connection was made at Towanda with the Barclay Railroad. During this year also ground was purchased and pockets erected sufficient for the transfer of 100,000 tons of coal at Waverly.

In this year Judge Packer was again elected to the presidency of the road, which office he has continued to hold to the present time.

On September 20th, 1869, the road of the P. &

N. Y. C. & R. R. Company was opened for business as far as Waverly, its northern terminus, the whole length from Wilkes-Barre being one hundred and five miles. This important event was hailed with evident satisfaction by the people of the northern portion of our own State, and by the citizens of Southern and Western New York, who have long looked with eager anxiety for the completion of a railroad from the anthracite coal-field of Wyoming to their homes by the route that nature seems to have made the most feasible and generally acceptable.

A fact of considerable interest may here be noted, viz., that in the construction of railroads in this section of country, the engineers' lines have generally been those of the old Indian war-paths, which would naturally prove to be the best suited for this purpose.

During this same year, the Lehigh Valley Railroad Company continued the policy approved by the stockholders at their previous annual meeting, of securing a proportion of the coal trade from each region by the purchase of interests in other companies owning lands on or near their several branches.

In October, a very disastrous flood occurred, doing more or less damage along the whole line of the road, and seriously impeding its business for a short period.

In this year the extensive car-, machine-, and repair-shops at Weatherly were completed.

To guard the Company's interests at Buffalo, and to provide facilities for transferring coal and other products to Lake vessels from the several roads entering that city, this Company subscribed to thirty-four-fortieths of the stock of the Buffalo Creek Railroad

Company, and commenced this year the work of construction, which was completed in June, 1870.

Arrangements were made in the latter part of 1870, by laying a third rail on the Erie Railway, by which trains now run through to Elmira over that road, and also to Auburn over the Southern Central Railroad of New York, with which latter road a connection is made at Athens. Thus an opening was made for the important trade on both the Erie and New York Central Railroads.

As a further protection to its coal trade, the Lehigh Valley Railroad Company this year secured a controlling interest in an additional quantity of coal lands.

During this year, the branch road, three and a half miles in length, from Slatington to Slatedale, was completed, furnishing much-needed facilities for the transportation of slate from the quarries. Several other branch roads to various collieries were also graded and laid; in addition to which, surveys and locations of lines were made for a prospective increase of coal tonnage in the Wyoming Valley.

The manufacture of steel rails (some of which, made abroad, had been laid down by the Company in 1864) in the United States being now an assured fact, contracts were made with several home companies for a considerable number of tons, every year's experience demonstrating the superiority of such rails over every other kind, as also of this metal when used for tires and fire-boxes.

The first year's business over the line of the Pennsylvania and New York Canal and Railroad Company more than realized the anticipations formed concerning it, the total earnings being $926,265.60, or, on an average, $8,673.24 per mile. The receipts of the Lehigh Valley Railroad the first year (1856) were $5,272.01 per mile. The receipts of the Canal were, in addition, $23,420.16, considerably less than the expenses of operating and repairs, which latter item was unusually large on account of damage from freshets.

The Company's coal trade had suffered for a number of years from the want of an independent outlet to tide-water, and to remedy this deficiency in part, a perpetual lease was made, early in 1871, of the property of the Morris Canal and Banking Company. By this arrangement, the Lehigh Valley Railroad Company came into the possession of a line of canal one hundred and two miles long, extending from the terminus of the road at Phillipsburg to Jersey City, with a basin of sixty acres, having a frontage of fifteen hundred feet on the North River, directly opposite New York City, and also of much valuable property at other points. One of the great advantages already resulting from this lease is the increased capacity for tonnage over the main line without material increase of rolling stock, in consequence of the ability to discharge the coal into the boats and return the cars at once to the mines.

In continuation of the policy alluded to above, a charter was obtained in the winter of 1871–72 from the Legislature of New Jersey for the Bound Brook and Easton Railroad Company, with authority to build a railroad from Easton to Bound Brook, which company, by an act passed later in the same session, was consolidated with the Perth Amboy and Bound Brook Railroad Company, under the name of the Easton and

Amboy Railroad Company. The stock of this consolidated company was almost entirely taken by, and its interests are now identical with those of, the Lehigh Valley Railroad Company.

A careful survey of the whole line from Phillipsburg to Perth Amboy has been made, and all the heavier parts of the work put under contract. Satisfactory progress is being made in its construction; the road may be in operation some time during the next year. It is also in contemplation to construct, at an early day, from some point on this same road, a direct and independent line to New York, for passengers and freight.

At Perth Amboy a large tract of valuable land has been secured, with a view to the construction of extensive wharves for the storage and shipping of the coal received, as well from the trade in general as from the mines already owned and controlled by the company. Plans for them have been adopted, and the wharves are already in course of erection.

During the year 1871 the Hazleton Branch, into the Valley of the Black Creek, was opened for about nine miles to a junction with the Danville, Hazleton and Wilkes-Barre Railroad, thus making in connection with that road an alternative route to Sunbury and intermediate points, and affording an eastern outlet for the business of the Philadelphia and Erie Railroad at Sunbury. A large body of valuable coal lands, heretofore undeveloped, will find a market for their produce over this extension.

In the latter part of 1870, Mr. John P. Cox, the Superintendent of the P. & N. Y. C. & R. R. Co.

(an official of many years' service and highly esteemed by a large circle of friends), died suddenly, and Mr. R. A. Packer was elected to fill the vacancy. The business of this road during the year was materially increased by the opening of the Sullivan and Erie Railroad, the Southern Central Railroad, and the Ithaca and Athens Railroad; the former principally as a feeder, and the two latter as outlets for coal. The completion of the narrow-gauge railroad between Tunkhannock and Montrose will also add very considerably to the traffic of this division of the road.

During the session of the Legislature in 1872, the Company was released from the obligation to maintain the canal, except that portion of it between the Feeder Dam on the Lackawanna River and Northampton Street, Wilkes-Barre, while this may be required to feed the canal between this latter place and Nanticoke Dam.

During the year 1872 a considerable increase of capital became necessary for the building of the Easton and Amboy Railroad and for the purchase of additional coal lands. To meet this need, a resolution was adopted authorizing a distribution of new stock to the stockholders in proportion of one share for every three shares then held, an opportunity which was fully embraced by those interested.

The equipment of the Lehigh Valley Railroad Company on the 30th of November, 1872, was as follows:

Engines of all classes	181
Passenger Cars	44
Baggage and Express Cars	25
Gravel Cars	69
Wreck and Tool Cars	9

Four-wheel Platform Cars	13
Four-wheel Caboose Cars	2
Eight-wheel Caboose Cars	16
House Cars	200
Eight-wheel Platform and Gondola Cars . .	600
Six-wheel Platform Cars	100
Lime Cars	44
Coal Cars (rated as four-wheel)	15,696

At the close of the Company's last fiscal year, November 30th, 1872, its capital account was as follows:

Preferred and Common Stocks (429,376 shares)	$21,468,800 00
Scrip for Instalments Received .	700,830 00
Hazleton Coal Co. Bonds (over due)	3,000 00
Bonds due in 1873	703,000 00
Six per cent. Bonds (Coupon and Registered), due in 1898	4,048,000 00
Seven per cent. Registered Bonds, due in 1910	5,000,000 00
Floating Debt, less cash on hand, none.	
Total	$31,923,630 00

The equipment of the P. & N. Y. C. & R. R. Company on the same date was as follows:

Locomotives	18
Passenger Cars	2
Flat and Gondola Cars	207
Box Cars	131
Stock Cars	50
Four-wheel Coal Cars	781
Gravel Cars	31
Four-wheel Caboose Cars	18
Eight-wheel Derrick Cars	2

And a supply of hand cars and small trucks necessary for repairs of road.

The road is well supplied with telegraphic communications, two wires running over the greater portion thereof, and a through wire from Philadelphia to Waverly. On November 30th, 1872, there were thirty-six offices and forty-eight sets of instruments.

Tabular Statement of the Tonnage, Receipts, and other Details of the Business of the Lehigh Valley Railroad from its opening to November 30th, 1872.

Year.	Coal Tonnage east of Mauch Chunk.	Total Coal Tonnage.	Total Receipts.	Net Receipts.	Gross Receipts, per Mile.	Loco-motives	Coal Cars.	Miles of Main Road.
1855 (3 Mos.)	8,482 16	8,482 16	$17,281 63	$7,050 45	$375 69	4		46
1856	165,740 00	165,740 00	242,512 61	98,928 65	5,272 01	10		46
1857	418,235 03	418,235 03	441,187 46	268,724 87	9,591 03	15	1,114	46
1858	471,029 10	471,029 10	442,045 35	247,371 59	9,609 68	15	1,117	46
1859	577,651 10	577,651 10	525,866 48	313,893 58	11,433 88	19	1,317	46
1860	730,641 17	730,641 17	679,908 59	342,039 54	14,780 61	21	1,473	46
1861	743,671 18	743,671 18	679,491 30	358,153 65	14,771 55	21	1,539	46
1862	882,573 14	882,573 14	856,054 53	448,501 71	18,609 88	28	1,797	46
1863	1,195,154 18	1,195,154 18	1,370,075 80	780,976 36	29,784 25	29	2,280	46
1864	1,295,419 02	1,466,794 02	2,411,917 69	1,406,782 15	27,723 19	53	5,099	87
1865	1,402,276 16	1,687,462 00	3,238,337 06	1,873,881 05	37,222 27	58	5,199	87
1866	1,730,474 12	2,037,714 07	3,711,574 73	1,963,010 23	29,225 00	86	6,441	127
1867	1,948,385 05	2,080,156 16	3,641,136 08	1,844,601 20	23,045 17	90	6,980	158
1868	2,225,630 02	2,603,102 11	4,270,649 70	1,769,356 01	22,596 03	117	9,084	189
1869	2,015,296 11	2,310,170 08	4,925,061 06	2,104,010 69	26,058 53	136	10,904	189
1870	2,810,020 07	3,608,586 13	5,938,167 48	2,320,760 10	30,609 11	158	12,729	194
1871	2,210,272 05	2,889,074 03	5,290,724 65	1,828,694 87	26,191 71	171	14,054	202
1872	3,009,395 11	3,850,118 09	5,982,949 48	2,113,262 50		181	15,696	202
TOTALS,	23,840,346 17	27,726,360 15	$44,664,941 68	$20,089,999 20	$29,618 66	181	15,696	202

Average Stock Dividends per year from opening of Road (17 years) . . $4\frac{84}{100}$ per cent.
Average Cash Dividends " " " " . . $7\frac{02}{100}$ "
Average Total Dividends " " " " . . $11\frac{86}{100}$ "

Earnings of the Pennsylvania and New York Canal and Railroad Company.

	1869.*		1870.		1871.		1872.	
	Railroad.	Canal.	Railroad.	Canal.	Railroad.	Canal.	Railroad.	Canal.
Coal—Anthracite .	$65,153 95		$524,676 53		†$783,005 28		$916,258 64	$2,805 08
" Bituminous .	41,018 46	$91,915 73	63,061 55	$23,420 26		$9,208 82	82,794 05	
Freight			200,510 27		314,981 94		399,477 57	
Pass., Mail & Express	79,600 35		135,426 96		172,634 92		183,051 64	
Miscellaneous . .			2,590 29		604 00		§26,705 07	
Total Earnings . .	$185,772 76	$91,915 73	$926,265 60	$23,420 26	$1,271,225 89	$9,208 82	$1,608,286 97	$2,805 08
Expenses	117,633 16	72,601 48	581,810 18	55,961 23	912,089 32	34,852 01	1,171,151 83	28,422 56
Net Earnings . .	$68,139 60	$19,314 25	$344,455 43	‡32,540 97	$359,136 57	‡$25,643 19	$437,135 14	‖$25,617 48
Total Net Earnings	$87,453 85		$311,914 45		$333,493 38		$411,517 66	

* Road unfinished. † Freight on Bituminous Coal included. ‡ Loss. § Including $25,628 57 from the Sullivan & Erie R. R. ‖ Loss.

Tonnage of the Pennsylvania and New York Canal and R. R. Co.

	Anthracite Coal.	Bituminous Coal.	Miscell's Freight.
*1869 . . .	284,609	165,679	11,151
1870 . . .	471,926	238,399	90,926
1871 . . .	415,194	302,262	177,621
1872 . . .	†671,484	336,555	215,124

* Road unfinished. † Including 90,547 by Canal for a short distance.

DISTANCES.

MAIN LINE.

NAMES OF STATIONS, AND MILES FROM

EASTON.

2 Glendon.
4 Chain Dam.
7 Redington.
9 Freemansburg.
12 Bethlehem.
17 East Penn Junction.
17 Allentown.
18 Furnace.
19 Ferndale.
20 Catasauqua.
21 Hokendauqua.
22 Coplay.
23 Portland.
24 White Hall.
26 Laury.
29 Rockdale.
33 Slatington.
35 Lehigh Gap.
38 Kittatinny.
39 Bowman's.
40 Parryville.
42 Lehighton.
44 Packerton.
46 Mauch Chunk.
46 East Mauch Chunk.
48 Glen Onoko.
52 Bear Creek.
53 Penn Haven Junction.

WYOMING DIVISION.

NAMES OF STATIONS, AND MILES FROM EASTON.

57 Stony Creek.
59 Drake's Creek.
61 Rock Port.
64 Mud Run.
66 Hickory Run.
69 Tannery.
71 White Haven.
77 Moosehead.
85 Fairview.
92 Newport.
95 Warrior Run.
97 Sugar Notch.
100 South Wilkes-Barre.
101 Wilkes-Barre.

PENNSYLVANIA AND NEW YORK CANAL AND RAILROAD.

NAMES OF STATIONS, AND MILES FROM EASTON.

106 Plainesville.
108 Port Blanchard.
110 Pittston.
111 L. & B. Junction.
116 Ransom.
122 Falls.
125 McKune.
128 La Grange.
133 Tunkhannock.
138 Vosburg.
145 Mehoopany.
148 Meshoppen.
153 Black Walnut.
155 Skinner's Eddy.

156 Laceyville.
166 Wyalusing.
172 Frenchtown.
176 Rummerfield.
179 Standing Stone.
183 Wysauking.
187 Towanda.
194 Ulster.
198 Milan.
202 Athens.
204 Sayre.
206 Waverly.

BEAVER MEADOW BRANCH.

NAMES OF STATIONS, AND MILES FROM EASTON.

54 Penn Haven.
60 Weatherly.
66 Beaver Meadow.
68 Leviston.
69 Jeanesville.
70 Audenried.

HAZLETON BRANCH.

NAMES OF STATIONS, AND MILES FROM EASTON.

62 Hazle Creek Bridge.
63 Miller's.
65 Lumber Yard.
66 Tunnel.
68 Eckley.
67 Foundry.
69 Jeddo.
71 Ebervale.
68 Stockton.
70 Hazleton.
71 Cranberry.
74 Conyngham.
78 Tomhicken.

MAHANOY BRANCH.

NAMES OF STATIONS, AND MILES FROM EASTON.

59 Black Creek Junction.
62 Hartz.
66 Gerhard.
71 Switch Back.
73 Quakake Junction.
77 Delano.
79 Meyersville.
81 Mahanoy City.
82 Yatesville.
84 Shenandoah.
89 Raven Run.
93 Centralia.
100 Mount Carmel.

CONNECTIONS.

At Easton with C. R. R. of N. J., for New York, Newark, Elizabeth, Plainfield, Somerville, and intermediate points.

At Phillipsburg with Morris and Essex R. R., for Schooley's Mountain, Hackettstown, Dover, Morristown, Newark, New York, and intermediate points.

With Belvidere Division of the Pennsylvania R. R., for Belvidere, Trenton, Philadelphia, and Stations on the New York Division.

At Bethlehem with North Pennsylvania R. R., for Philadelphia, Baltimore, and Washington.

At East Penn Junction with Philadelphia and Reading R. R., for Reading, Pottsville, Lebanon, Harrisburg, Pittsburg, and the West.

At Catasauqua with Catasauqua and Fogelsville Railroad.

At Penn Haven Junction with Mahanoy, Beaver Meadow, and Hazleton Branches of the L. V. R. R.

At Quakake with Catawissa R. R., for Danville, Milton, Williamsport, Lock Haven, and Erie.

At Tomhicken with the Danville, Hazleton and Wilkes-Barre R. R., for Catawissa, Danville, Sunbury, etc.

At L. & B. Junction for Scranton.

At Athens with Southern Central R. R., for Owego, Auburn, also with Ithaca and Athens R. R., for Spencer, Vannettenville, etc., for the Cayuga, Lake Ithaca and Geneva R. R., and all points on the New York Central R. R.

At Elmira with Erie Railway, for Buffalo, Niagara, the Canadas, the West and Northwest, and with the Northern Central Railway for Watkins.

SKETCHES,

DESCRIPTIVE AND HISTORICAL,

OF THE

CITIES AND TOWNS ON THE ROUTE

OF THE

LEHIGH VALLEY RAILROAD,

ITS CONNECTIONS AND BRANCHES.

PHILLIPSBURG.

This town, although in New Jersey, deserves a place in this Guide, as being the present southern or eastern terminus of the Lehigh Valley Railroad. It was originally an Indian settlement, the site having been mapped as early as the year 1654. Its name is derived, as some would contend, from an old and influential chief of that name who resided there. Others ascribe its origin to a large landholder by the name of Phillips. The building of the New Jersey Central Railroad in 1852, and of the Belvidere Delaware Railroad in 1854, gave a decided impetus to the growth of the town, large sales of land being effected, which led to the organization of several extensive manufacturing establishments, for which it is advantageously located, surrounded as it is by a rich and fertile country, and possessed of ample railroad and canal facilities.

The railroad bridge connecting Phillipsburg with Easton is a double-track wooden bridge, built in 1866. Both tracks are on the same level. It connects at Phillipsburg with the Morris and Essex R.R., the Central R.R. of N. J., the works of the Morris Canal Co., and a branch of the Belvidere and Delaware R.R., the grade of which descends to a point near the Andover Iron Works, where it connects with the main line. The chief manufactories are a sheet-iron rolling-mill, bar-iron and carriage-axles rolling-mill, agricultural works, stove works, iron furnaces (the particulars of which are given below), the Warren Foundry and Machine Works, celebrated for their excellent quality of gas- and water-pipes (the capacity of which is twenty thousand tons per year), the works of the Phillipsburg Manufacturing Co. for the manufacture of iron bridges (capacity four thousand tons per year), and the Vulcanized Iron Works. Besides these, there are other industrial works, employing a great many hands.

It has a population of about 7000 people, and contains 1 Episcopal, 2 Methodist, 1 Presbyterian, 1 Lutheran, and 1 Roman Catholic church. It also has one national bank, with a capital of $200,000, and one savings bank; one weekly and one daily newspaper.

The works of the Andover Iron Company (capital, $750,000) consist of three stacks.

No. 1, 55 feet high, 18 feet bosh.
No. 2, 55 " " " "
No. 3, 42 " " " "

Their combined capacity is 32,000 tons of pig-iron

per annum. Including those employed in the ore mines, 400 men are in the service of the company.

Like its opposite neighbor, Easton (with which it is connected by several bridges), Phillipsburg is on a high elevation, and presents a commanding appearance.

EASTON, PENNSYLVANIA.

This town is one of the oldest in the State, having been laid out in 1750, and its early history is replete with interesting details. It is situated at the junction of the Delaware, Lehigh, and Bushkill Rivers, in part upon the débris which their waters have washed down and lodged here. Its name was given by Thomas Penn from his friend Lord Pomfret's house. The name of the new county (it having been formerly a part of Bucks) was also the suggestion of Penn. Its records reveal a steady growth and improvement in all essential particulars. It was incorporated as a borough in 1789, and received a second charter of incorporation in 1823. Its streets are regularly laid out, and either paved or macadamized, and are lighted with gas, supplied with water, and kept very neat and clean. The public green, called the "Circle," from its form, is handsomely inclosed and shaded. Many houses, including a number of fine residences, have been built upon the neighboring hills, giving the town a romantic appearance.

The court-house, built of limestone, rough-cast, occupies a commanding position on a hill in the western part of the town, and is an imposing structure, erected at a cost of $60,000. To the north are the house and grounds of the Farmers' and Mechanics'

Institute (said to be the finest in the State), where the county fairs are held annually. There are also several public halls, and the following church buildings: 4 Lutheran, 2 Presbyterian, 2 German Reformed, and 1 each of Baptist, Methodist Episcopal, German Methodist, Protestant Episcopal, Bethel Mission, Roman Catholic, and a Jewish Synagogue. An Opera House capable of seating fifteen hundred persons has been erected during the past year.

There are two daily newspapers (one, the "Express," being the pioneer in this part of the country), and four weekly.

The citizens take great pride in their public schools, thinking them without any superiors in the State in point of a well-graded system, buildings, and playgrounds. Recently, there has been erected a very complete and handsome new school-house, constructed of red sandstone trimmed with Ohio sandstone, at a cost of over $100,000.

There are also six private schools for both sexes, foremost among which is Lafayette College, for young men, which is under the patronage of the Presbyterian Church. This institution was chartered in 1826, shortly after the visit of the Marquis de Lafayette to America. After remaining for some time in a humble building, the corner-stone of the main building of the series now standing was laid in 1833. This series comprises a number of handsome and substantial structures used for educational purposes (including Jenks Hall, a new observatory,—built at the expense of Prof. Traill Green,—and a recent addition of a large wing to the main edifice), and as residences of the

Faculty. The grounds cover an area of forty acres, and the value of the real estate (exclusive of apparatus, worth $20,000, and extensive collections in mineralogy) is estimated at $220,000. There is at interest as an endowment fund nearly $300,000, including a munificent donation of $200,000 from A. Pardee, Esq., of Hazleton, who has lately made another donation of $200,000 for the erection of a building (now in progress) designed for the departments of Engineering, Metallurgy, and Chemistry. Its curriculum of study includes all the branches suited to a liberal, classical, and scientific education, and, with its able Faculty, very few colleges offer greater inducements. There are rooms in the college buildings provided for one hundred and forty students, and additional private accommodations can be secured at moderate prices. There were for the year 1872 two hundred and forty-three students in actual attendance, and a corps of twenty-six professors and tutors.

There is a well-maintained public library (founded in 1811), containing about 5000 volumes.

The Easton Cemetery is a lovely spot of thirty acres, on the Bushkill, containing many beautiful and costly monuments, including one to George Taylor, one of the signers of the Declaration of Independence, whose grave is unknown, but whose dwelling (a plain two-story stone building) is still standing, opposite the new public school-house.

While Easton proper can have but few large manufactories, owing to the peculiar situation of the town, yet the water-power of the Bushkill has been extensively used by saw-mills, foundries, tanneries, sash-factories, planing-mills, paint-works, forge for carriage-axles, etc. There is also a steam rope-walk, 1100 feet long. The wholesale and retail stores do a very large buiness, supplying the country for many miles round. A sheet-iron rolling-mill has lately been erected, with a capacity of about 15 tons per week.

There are two national banks, each having a capital of $400,000, in addition to which there are two savings-banks, with a combined capital of $145,000.

Several earnest attempts have been made at different periods to navigate the Delaware as far as Easton, with steamboats especially constructed for this purpose, but always without any permanent success.

The town is situated in the midst of a rich mineral region, and presents a large variety of interesting fields for exploration. At the Phillipsburg Cut, on the south, the limestone and granite (the only instance of this latter mineral being found in this region) come together,—an unusual occurrence. The scenery in the neighborhood is very picturesque. From Mount Taylor and Chestnut Hill, each about 800 feet high, very fine views can be obtained. From the latter (about a mile north of Easton) a bold isolated rock projects to a height of 258 feet, containing a profile of an Indian chief's head, hence called St. Anthony's Nose.

A fine covered bridge (a combination of the truss and arch principle), 600 feet long, erected in 1805, at a cost of over $60,000, for carriage and foot travel, crosses the Delaware to Phillipsburg, and has been remarkably preserved during the many severe freshets common to this locality. An iron bridge across the Lehigh connects Easton and South Easton, between which towns a horse-car railroad runs. Over this, and crossing diagonally, the Lehigh and Susquehanna Railroad Company have constructed a very long and substantial iron bridge to connect with the New Jersey railroads.

Population, about 11,000.

SOUTH EASTON.

This town was founded by the Lehigh Coal and Navigation Company in 1833, and incorporated as a borough in 1840. Its water-powers are derived from the canal of that Company, which debouches at this place by outlet locks into the basin at the mouth of the Lehigh. This power propels a grist-mill, a large cotton-mill of nearly three hundred looms, employing 200 hands, and manufacturing tickings, osnaburgs, and stripes; the Glendon Iron Company's Works (for an account of which, see GLENDON); and Stewart's Wire and Rolling Mill, which latter establishment is one of the oldest of its kind in the country, dating back to 1836. It employs 150 hands, its capacity is 20 tons per day, and it makes nearly all varieties of bright and annealed wire.

Here are located extensive shops belonging to the Lehigh Valley Railroad Company, employing about 200 hands, and (besides repairs) manufacturing cars, frogs, switches, and road-equipments generally. A number of superior locomotives have also been turned out hence within a few years past, which compare most favorably with any that are in use through the Valley.

The dimensions of the various buildings are as follows:

New boiler-shop	45 by 90 feet.
Machine-shop	300 by 60 "
Car-shop	125 by 36 "
Blacksmith- and hammer-shop . .	160 by 40 "
Old boiler-shop	50 by 60 "
Store-room	30 by 80 "
Foundry	40 by 80 "
Round-house	200 feet in diameter,

with accommodations for 28 engines.

During the year 1872, the Foundry produced of—

Some cast iron	1,354,870 lbs.
" cast brass	27,784 "

and consumed of—

Pig-iron	600 tons.
Merchant iron	175 "
Cast scrap iron	40 "
Pig copper	15,000 lbs.
Amount of material used	$240,000

During the same period, sixty-four locomotives and sixty-seven passenger and baggage cars were repaired at these shops.

There are 3 churches, German Roman Catholic, Methodist, and Lutheran, a public school-house, and a town hall. Population, 3500.

GLENDON.

Here are the extensive works of the Glendon Iron Company for the manufacture of pig-iron. Including one (No. 4) at South Easton, there are five stacks in all, with the following dimensions and capacity:

No. 1, 16 feet boshes,	50 feet high,	220 tons per week.
" 2, 14 " "	50 " "	195 " " "
" 3, 16 " "	50 " "	220 " " "
" 4, 15 " "	47 " "	195 " " "
" 5, 18 " "	72 " "	310 " " "

The company is a stock one, with a capital of $1,000,000. Excluding 150 men engaged in the mines, 400 men are employed in these works. The hæmatite ore and limestone are obtained in the immediate neighborhood, the magnetic ore from Morris and Sussex Counties, New Jersey; and this holds true of nearly all the furnaces along the Lehigh.

The amount of material consumed yearly by this company is as follows:

Iron ore	100,000 tons.
Coal	85,000 "
Limestone	50,000 "

Producing from 55,000 to 57,000 tons of pig-iron.

Recently, the Easton Iron and Manufacturing Company have erected here a furnace with a stack 72 feet high and bosh 18 feet wide, the capacity of which is 200 tons per week. The whole population of the town is between 600 and 700, with two school-houses, but no church.

Another furnace is about to be erected by the Keystone Iron Company at Chain Dam, about a mile above Glendon.

REDINGTON.

Formerly called Lime Ridge, from the quantity of limestone abounding in this locality. The scenery at this point of the river is particularly beautiful. The Coleraine Iron Company have recently erected here two stacks 18 by 60 and 17 by 60 feet respectively, with a capacity of 500 tons per week, and giving employment to nearly 200 men, some of whom are engaged in the foundry and machine-shop.

FREEMANSBURG.

This pretty and thriving borough, named after Mr. Jacob Freeman, was settled in 1830, was incorporated in 1854, and contains three boat-yards (where in the busiest seasons about 100 boats are made per annum), saw- and grist-mills, and a soap and candle factory. There are two churches, one Evangelical and one used in common by the Lutherans and the German Reformed. The Northampton Iron Company (capital $250,000) have lately erected here a furnace 65 feet high and 16 feet bosh, having a capacity of 200 tons per week. They employ about 100 hands. Population about 800. The Shinersville Grist Mill was built in 1745, and is the oldest in Northampton county.

It was at a short distance above Freemansburg that the Indian path passed the Lehigh upon which the famous walk was performed in 1737. In the summer of that year the Indians agreed, in pursuance of a former unfulfilled contract with William Penn, to grant as much land north of where Wrightstown, in Bucks County, now stands as would be included in a walk of a day and a half. The Proprietaries, Thomas and John Penn, at once advertised for three expert walkers, one of whom, Edward Marshall, accomplished a distance of seventy-four miles within the given time, ending his walk on a spur of the Second or Broad Mountain.

The Indians were very much dissatisfied and exasperated at the result of the walk, denouncing it as a fraud, in which view of the case many of the white settlers coincided. Pamphlets were published by both parties, criminating and recriminating each other

THE GEM OF THE VALLEY.
(From Freemansburg looking North.)

Page 38.

BETHLEHEM.

Page 39.

upon the subject. The Indians and the whites became involved finally in a war, which lasted from 1755 to 1758, during which many cruel murders were committed, but the Indians were at length compelled to yield the territory.

Just above the depot, the Saucon creek empties into the Lehigh, after draining a very rich valley.

BETHLEHEM.

This name is commonly given to two separate boroughs. Bethlehem proper is situated on the north side of the Lehigh. The railroad station is in what is legally South Bethlehem, situated on the south side of the Lehigh, the terminus also of the North Pennsylvania Railroad, leading to Philadelphia. We will, for convenience' sake, consider them as one settlement. A peculiar interest has always attached to the town, from the fact of its having been the principal settlement of the Moravians, or United Brethren, in the United States. They came to the New World early in its history, to attempt the conversion of the Indians to Christianity. They first settled in Georgia; but in 1738 their settlement was broken up on account of the war then raging between England and Spain, and their attention was directed to Pennsylvania. For an entire century they retained here some of their distinctive principles, viz., the separation of sexes, the "family-house" arrangements, the exclusion of all persons who were not members of their church, etc. Of late years, these peculiar characteristics have more and more ceased to be noticeable, and the influx of strangers has partially removed the former quaint and foreign appearance of the town.

Some additional historic interest attaches to this place, from the fact that Washington, in his retreat across the Delaware, was compelled to remove his hospital and supplies to Bethlehem,—the Moravians giving him the use of their buildings, which at one time were filled by British prisoners. Thus the town came to be honored by the presence of Washington, Adams, Lafayette, Pulaski, Gates, Hancock, and Franklin.

Washington, we are told, supplied himself with domestic goods from the Sisters' House, selecting "blue stripes" for his wife, and stout woolen hose for himself. It was in the spring of 1778, when detachments of the American army passed through Bethlehem, and some of the choir-houses were converted into barracks, hospitals, and places of safe-keeping for English prisoners, that Count Pulaski was complimented for his gallantry by the presentation of a banner, embroidered by the single Sisters, as a token of gratitude for the protection he had afforded them. The banner was received by him gratefully, and borne in his regiment through the campaign, until he fell in the attack upon Savannah, in the autumn of 1779. It is now carefully preserved in the hall of the Maryland Historical Society, at Baltimore. Longfellow has made this incident the subject of a highly-wrought poem.

The name of the town took its origin at the time of the first Christmas-eve service, which was held in the year 1741, partly in a stable in the rear of the Eagle Hotel. At first the name was Beth-Lecha, meaning the house by the river Lecha. Afterwards, on account of the service, it was changed, it is said at the suggestion of Count Zinzendorf, to that which now prevails. The old buildings, for the most part, still remain, and are objects of curious interest to the many tourists who frequent the town. The principal ones stand upon Church Street. Among them may be mentioned the church, a large and chaste-looking edifice, kept, as are all their buildings, in excellent repair; the old chapel, built in 1751, and still used for religious services; the Congregation's House, where was the original chapel and residence of the clergy; the Sisters' and Widows' Houses, wherein infirm and aged women find a comfortable home, and which still preserve their primitive interior arrangement, such as broad oaken staircases, flagged pavements, small windows, and low ceilings. The graveyard is also kept as heretofore, one of its peculiarities consisting in the uniform plain slab covering the remains of poor and rich alike, bearing only the impartial records of their life. Nisky Hill, where new and beautiful cemetery-grounds have been laid out, forms one of the pleasantest walks that the town affords. The island in the Lehigh is much resorted to in the proper season for picnics and excursions.

Besides the 3 Moravian church buildings, there are churches belonging to the following denominations: 2 Reformed, 2 Episcopal, 3 Methodist, 2 Roman Catholic, and 3 Lutheran. The Hall of the Young Men's Christian Association and Citizen's Hall are neat and substantial buildings, much used for concerts and lectures,—the people of Bethlehem being justly celebrated for their high appreciation of, and skill in, music, and the fine arts generally.

In addition to the public schools, the Moravians have an extensive day-school in a commodious building,

4*

intended chiefly for their own children. The boarding-school for girls—for scholars of any denomination—was first opened on the 5th of January, 1749, and has since grown to such dimensions as to require for its accommodation a suite of large buildings, to which additions are constantly made. The average number of pupils in attendance there is about 200, representing nearly all the States in the Union. Its graduates number over 5000, the Moravians having always been peculiarly successful in educating those intrusted to their charge.

The largest manufacturing establishment here is that of the Bethlehem Iron Company, including within its operations, which began in January, 1863, furnaces, rolling-mills, machine-shop, and foundry. Its capital stock is $1,000,000. The measurement of the three stacks is as follows: No. 1, 15 by 63 feet; No. 2, 15 by 45 feet; No. 3, 14 by 50 feet. Their combined capacity is about 30,000 tons per annum, the largest part of which is used in the adjoining rolling-mill, whose capacity is 20,000 tons per annum. Its consumption of raw materials is 70,000 tons of Pennsylvania hæmatite and New Jersey magnetic ore, and from 70,000 to 75,000 tons of coal. The total number of men employed at the works proper is about 700. The new building now erecting for the manufacture of iron and steel will be, it is said, the largest in this country, and one of the largest in existence anywhere. It will be 105 feet wide, spanned by an iron and slate roof without supporters. It is 30 feet high to the eaves, and is in the shape of a double cross, of which the long arm (or main building) is 931 feet, and the short arms

140½ feet each, making the area covered 1493 feet by 105 feet. This is only surpassed by the mill at Creuzot, in France, which consists of three buildings 60 by 1400 feet each.

The steel-works will start with a capacity of about 600 tons rails per week, planned and arranged for a threefold increase of the same.

There will be three trains of rolls, say 24, 26, and 30 inch diameters, driven by two condensing-engines of 48 and 56 inches diameter cylinders, of 46 and 48 inches stroke.

The mill will be remarkable not only for its enormous size and capacity, but for the many new labor-saving conveniences introduced.

The iron-work for the building, as well as the machinery, was all made at the company's shops and foundry.

The works of the Lehigh Zinc Company are also on a very large scale, employing as they do 700 men, including those in the mines, which are located at Friedensville, four miles south. The first discovery of zinc on the property now owned and worked by this company was made by Prof. Roepper in 1845. Now about 20,000 tons of both blende and earthy ore are mined in a year. The company was organized in 1849, and has now a capital of $1,000,000. It is engaged in the manufacture of spelter or metallic zinc, for which it has twenty-four Belgian furnaces yielding 700 pounds each in every twenty-four hours. A portion of this is converted into sheet zinc. The works for the manufacture of white oxide are 1390 square feet of grate surface, and yield about 3500 tons per annum. Here was the beginning of the manufacture of these articles in America, and it is thought that its products are very near in quality to the best imported. Its annual consumption of coal is about 30,000 tons. A brief description of the process of manufacture may be interesting.

The ore after being crushed fine is mixed with fine coal in the proportion of 50 pounds of coal to 100 pounds of ore, and in this condition is put into open furnaces, where the zinc is liberated in a gaseous form. The oxide of zinc, which is used for paint, is formed by forcing cold air through the mass of coal and ore in the furnace, which drives the gaseous zinc through various arrangements until it falls into long muslin bags, in the shape of a pure white powder. After again passing through bolting-cloths, it is ready for market. The metallic zinc is made by excluding the air when it is in a gaseous state. Such of the spelter as is to be rolled into sheet zinc is remelted and run into ingots of the proper size, and, at a moderate heat, passed through the rolls. The process of rolling into sheets is very similar to that employed in rolling sheet iron, except that it takes rather longer and is a more delicate operation.

One of the great difficulties which the company has had to encounter in working its mines, is the large amount of water which must be kept under control. To obviate it, various expedients have been resorted to, drains, pumps, engines, etc., until, the resources and endurance of the company being wellnigh exhausted, its engineer, Mr. John West, matured a plan of raising 15,000 gallons of water per minute from 300 feet depth, and late in 1871 the new engine, pumps, and shaft needed for this purpose were put into successful operation. The engine was made by Messrs. Merrick, of Philadelphia, the pumps, boilers, and mountings by Messrs. I. P. Morris & Co., of the same city. The timber for shaft and pump-rods was contracted for in Georgia.

The engine (which was three years in building) has a pumping capacity of 15,000 gallons per minute, and may be run to 17,000 in case of emergency, raising water from a depth of 300 feet. It weighs 657 tons, and, including the pumps and boilers, the total weight of the machinery is 1000 tons. Size of cylinder, 110¼ inches in diameter; length of stroke, 10 feet; estimated at 3000 horse-power. The bob wall of solid masonry, 9 feet thick, was commenced on a plat of solid rock, 114 feet below the surface; the foundation for the engine is 32 feet deep below the bed-plate. The heaviest pieces of iron in the engine are the sections of beams, and weigh 24 tons. There are two pieces of wrought-iron weighing 16 tons each. The fly-wheels weigh 75 tons each; crank-pins 1 ton each. The piston-rod is 14 inches in diameter. The crosshead weighs 8 tons. The connecting-rods have 9-inch necks, and are 15 inches in the middle, 41 feet 2½ inches long, and weigh 11 tons each. There are two air-pumps, 50 inches in diameter each.

The work of "The President" (so far as known, the most powerful stationary engine in the world) is at present to drive two plunger pumps, each 30 inches in diameter by 10 feet stroke. They will throw 735 gallons per stroke. The engine can work comfortably at 12 strokes per minute, and the power is more than adequate, and the dimensions of the shaft (30½ by 21½ feet in the clear) ample for doubling this number of pumps, and carrying all to a depth of 300 feet, or 178 feet below the present bottom of the mines, with power still in reserve for what may be required below.

In addition to its other works, the company has a cooper-shop run by the water-power of the canal, with a capacity of 20,000 casks per year.

Besides these establishments, there are brass-works (manufacturing valves, cocks, whistles, cups, lubricators, etc.), flour-mills, shovel-factory, barrel-factory, carriage-factories, etc. There are published here three weekly and two daily newspapers.

By the Lehigh and Lackawanna Railroad, direct communication has been opened with the extensive slate quarries at Bath and Chapman's. There are two national banks, with a combined capital of $800,000, besides which there are two savings banks with a combined capital of $36,000. Both boroughs are well supplied with water and gas, and are growing rapidly in population, which now numbers nearly 10,000. Many handsome residences have been erected on both sides of the river, and the continuous importance and prosperity of the towns as a business and educational centre seem now to be well assured. It has been for a number of years a favorite place of resort for travelers, and the points of interest hitherto attracting them are largely on the increase.

South Bethlehem is the seat of the *Lehigh University*, which was formally opened on September 1st, 1866. It was founded by the Hon. Asa Packer, of Mauch Chunk, President of the Lehigh Valley Railroad, who appropriated to this object the sum of $500,000 and a very eligible tract of land containing fifty-six acres, in addition to which he has subsequently made liberal donations at various times. The system adopted here, while it does not ignore the classics, proposes to give particular attention to those branches of a liberal or polytechnic education which tend to develop the vast resources of the country, such as Engineering, Chemistry, Metallurgy, Architecture, and Construction. Its situation among the many industrial works surrounding Bethlehem is especially adapted for securing to the student such a practical education. Through the generosity of the founder, and by a resolution of the Trustees, passed in July, 1871, tuition was declared to be hereafter *free* in all branches and classes. The personal expenses of the student need not exceed two hundred and fifty dollars per year.

For the year 1872–3 there were 13 professors and instructors, and 120 students. While the University is under the auspices of the Episcopal Church, no undue influence is brought to bear upon the students contrary to their own religious predilections or the express wishes of their parents. *Packer Hall*, the principal University building, is of stone, 213 feet long, and is one of the handsomest and completest college edifices in the country. It is built on a gentle declivity of the Lehigh Mountain range, in the midst of a park of forest-trees, and commands a beautiful and unobstructed view for twenty miles. Near it are erected the observatory, houses for the President and professors, and *Christmas Hall*, a commodious brick building containing rooms for boarders, etc.

The Episcopalians have also, admirably situated a short distance from the depot, a promising girls' boarding-school, called *Bishopthorpe*, where a thorough education is given.

The offices of the Superintendent and Assistant General Superintendent of the Company, and of the President's Assistant, are located in this borough, in commodious buildings adjoining the depot.

EAST PENN JUNCTION.

The station here is the junction of the East Penn Railroad, extending to Reading, Harrisburg, Pittsburg, and thence to the Great West, the shortest and most favorable route thither from New York.

Near by are the blast-furnaces of the Lehigh Iron Company, with a capital of $500,000, and employing over 250 men at their works, mines, and quarries. They consume annually about 35,000 tons of coal, 49,000 tons of ore, and 26,000 tons of limestone. Their disbursements for labor and materials amount to about $720,000 per annum. Their motive power consists of two large condensing steam engines with a combined capacity of over 1000 horse-power. The works produce per annum about 22,000 tons of foundry and forge pig-iron. The office of the company is at Allentown, and is connected with the furnaces by their own telegraph wire.

ALLENTOWN.

This city is situated at the junction of the Lehigh River with the Little Lehigh and Jordan Creek. The Jordan runs through the northern part of the town. The eminence upon which the town is built commands an unusually beautiful prospect, sloping gradually to the river on the east, and to the creek on the north. It derives its name, some say, from James Allen, who laid it out in 1762. Others say it derives its name from William Allen, the father of James, who was a particular friend of the Penn family, from whom he inherited large tracts of land. He was one of the most distinguished citizens of Philadelphia, having been for a number of years Chief Justice of the Supreme Court of Pennsylvania. The Greenleaf family at one time owned nearly the whole of the ground now comprised within the city limits. During the war of the Revolution, among many valuable articles from Philadelphia which were concealed here, was the chime belonging to Christ Church of that city. Originally the town was known as Northampton, as is stated in the assessment list from 1762 to 1800, where its present name is first found. In 1826 it was incorporated with its former name, and it was not until 1838 that it reassumed the name of Allentown. It was chartered as a city in 1867. The town for many years did not progress very rapidly, owing mainly, perhaps, to the difficulty (because of its elevation) of procuring the necessary supply of water for domestic purposes. A great fire in 1848 gave a temporary shock to its prosperity, but was eventually the means of infusing new life into the town, a much finer set of buildings taking the place of those destroyed. The completion of the Lehigh Valley and East Penn Railroads gave great impetus to its growth.

It now presents a beautiful and substantial appearance. The streets are laid out at right angles, and are broad and clean, adorned with shade-trees, and well lighted with gas. The main street, Hamilton, is built up for a mile and a half. In the heart of the town is a large square, which is the centre of a very extensive business. Within a few years, there have been erected a number of handsome private residences, many of which are surrounded with large and beautiful gardens. A street railway runs from the depot to the principal parts of the city. The scenery and natural curiosities of the city and neighborhood are well worth seeing. The view from the Big or Bauer's Rock, near by (about 1000 feet high), is very extensive and picturesque, embracing as it does a rich variety of landscape and industry in both the Saucon and Lehigh Valleys. There are several romantic springs in the neighborhood, much resorted to by strangers. One of these supplies the city with water, and another—four miles distant—turns a saw-mill and grist-mill immediately at the place at which it issues from the ground. It also forms Cedar Creek, upon which there are a large number of mills, to accommodate whose business an extension of the railroad is contemplated. A number of trout are raised upon this stream. A very substantial and tasteful iron bridge has lately been erected over the Lehigh, while the stone one crossing the Jordan Creek and leading into the main street is perhaps the largest structure of the kind in Pennsylvania. It consists of 19 arches, is about 1800 feet long, and 50 feet high, and cost originally $20,000.

Allentown has many advantages as a manufacturing town. Its situation in the midst of a rich agricultural district; its nearness to valuable beds of iron ore, zinc, limestone, cement, etc.; its railroad and canal accommodations, and the peculiarly favorable sites for manufactories, all point it out as the seat of one of the largest cities in Pennsylvania. The population is over 15,000.

Its chief industrial establishments are those of the Allentown Rolling-Mill Company, a stock company with a capital of $2,000,000 ($1,000,000 paid up) and employing nearly 1000 men. It has in the various departments of manufacture five trains of three high rolls, and three of two high rolls. It uses almost exclusively the pig-iron made in its own furnaces, and has a capacity of 20,000 tons per annum. In the year 1871, it used of pig-iron 17,000 tons, of old rails 5500 tons, and of coal 27,000 tons. The company is now erecting additional rolling-mills, to manufacture 30,000 tons rails, 4000 tons bar-iron, 400 tons bolts, nuts, etc. In the new mill, now nearly completed, steel head-rails for mines will be made. It also manufactures engines and other machinery. The company has lately bought out the Roberts Iron Company, having two stacks, measuring respectively 15 by 61½ feet and 15 by 67 feet, with a capacity of 17,000 tons of pig-iron per annum. It has also purchased the machine-shops of Thayer, Erdman, Wilson & Co., and the Lehigh Rolling Mill.

The Allentown Iron Works,—a stock company. Capital, $800,000. This company has five furnaces, with size and capacity as follows:

No. 1, 16 feet boshes,	60 feet high,	200 tons per week.
" 2, 16 " "	60 " "	200 " " "
" 3, 16 " "	60 " "	200 " " "
" 4, 14 " "	60 " "	200 " " "
" 5, 17 " "	60 " "	250 " " "

The company employs 600 men. It obtains its ore from Berks and Lehigh Counties, and from New Jersey.

Fire-Brick Works. Employ about 50 men, and produce about 1,800,000 bricks per annum, used chiefly by the works in the neighborhood. The clay comes from South Amboy, New Jersey.

Cole, Heilman & Brown's Boiler Shops. Employ 60 men in making stacks, boilers, tanks, etc.

There are also several other rolling-mills (the Glen, Hope, Jordan, etc.), foundries, and machine-shops, steam-forge, spike-works, brass-works, woolen-mills, planing-mills, carriage- and wagon-factories, mowing-machine-works, sash-factories, and other branches of manufactures. In addition to which, there is a very large wholesale and retail business done at the various stores.

There are three national banks, with an aggregate capital of $1,050,000, beside several savings-banks (with an authorized capital of $710,000) and private banking-houses.

The new county jail is one of the handsomest and most complete structures of the kind in the State. It is built mostly of Potsdam sandstone, and cost nearly $250,000. The court-house, erected several years ago at a cost of $60,000, is also in good keeping with the other public buildings. The Academy of Natural Sciences has lately been formed, and possesses a considerable library and cabinet.

Allentown has long been justly celebrated for the interest taken in educational matters by its citizens. This has been manifested in the establishment of numerous public schools of the highest order, which have been supported in the most liberal manner. Recently there have been erected two beautiful school-houses, constructed of sandstone, and arranged and furnished after the most approved models, one costing $70,000 and the other $60,000. A third new one, of brick, and complete in all its parts and appointments, lately built, cost $52,000. In the city, which is a separate school district, there are 56 teachers and 3150 scholars.

Among the private educational establishments, the foremost is Muhlenburg College, first founded in 1848, but re-established under new and favorable auspices in 1867. Two-thirds of the trustees are elected by the stockholders, and one-third by the Evangelic Lutheran Synod. The buildings of the institution (in which the accommodations are of the most approved character) are eligibly situated in the southeastern part of the city, surrounded by about five acres of ground, devoted to its exclusive use. They present a front of 120 feet, with a centre building of 50 feet, and two wings each of 35 feet. In front there is a fine lawn adorned with shade-trees, and in the rear a large campus supplied with a gymnasium. Pupils are admitted as they are found qualified into their proper departments of study, which embrace all those branches which are deemed essential to a thorough education. During the year ending June, 1873, there were in attendance 135 students, and the Faculty and instructors numbered 9.

The Allentown Female College occupies a beautiful and healthful site in the northeastern portion of the city, with ample buildings well ordered in all their apartments. The course of instruction is divided into

5*

Primary, Academic, and Collegiate, and is meant to include all the principal branches of a liberal education. During the past year, there were 82 scholars in attendance, and a board of 9 instructors.

There are 3 Lutheran, 3 German Evangelical, 2 Episcopal, 2 Reformed, and 2 Roman Catholic churches, and 1 belonging to each of the following denominations: 2 Baptist, 2 Methodist, Presbyterian, and 2 United Brethren.

The Fair Grounds contain twelve acres. The Floral Hall is built in four wings from a centre; each wing is one hundred feet long and two stories high. The lower part is for vegetable and floral display; the upper part is for domestic manufactures. The race-track is one-third of a mile around. There are stalls for one hundred head of horses and cattle. Average number of exhibitors, 1000; average entries, 4000; average annual attendance, 40,000; average receipts, $7000; average premium list, $3500. Water-pipes are laid through the grounds and buildings. The number of life-members is about 800. The fairs held here, which were the first established in the Lehigh Valley, dating back to 1852, are, as may be judged from these statistics, among the most successful in any part of the country.

The Opera House is a very fine building, 60 feet wide and 120 feet deep, three stories high; besides which there are other public buildings, Odd-Fellows' and Masonic halls, etc.

There are nine or ten papers published here, in both the German and English languages (among them two dailies and several religious magazines), with a large and increasing circulation.

CATASAUQUA.

This town takes its name from the creek which here empties into the river, and whose signification is *parched land.* In 1839 there were but two houses, one at each extreme end of the town plot. During that year, a company of gentlemen, mostly of Philadelphia, proposed the erection here (because of the proximity of the iron and limestone beds) of an iron furnace for the purpose of making iron with anthracite coal, which had been successfully accomplished in Wales a few years before by Mr. George Crane. The services of Mr. David Thomas, who was engaged there with Mr. Crane, were secured, and in 1840 the first furnace was completed under his direction and superintendence. Since then, the town has steadily progressed, until now it bids fair to become one of the most important in the Valley. It is located in the midst of a rich iron-ore and limestone region, and possesses unusual railroad and canal facilities, thus marking it out as a peculiarly favorable opening for manufacturing establishments. It was incorporated as a borough in 1853, and contains a population of 6000. The town is well supplied with gas and water, and few places can boast of so perfect a drainage. It has twelve public schools, contained in four buildings, and comprising about 700 pupils. Its high-school will compare favorably with any in the State. It has a fine town-hall, erected at a cost of $15,000. On the western bank of the river, opposite the borough, there is a beautiful cemetery, called "Fair-View," commanding a magnificent view of the town and surrounding country. In it there has been erected a very handsome marble monument to the memory of the soldiers who fell in the late civil war, costing $6000.

In enumerating the industrial works coming properly under the head of Catasauqua, we include not only those actually located in the borough, but all, whether on one side of the river or the other, stretching from Allentown Furnace to this station.

The Crane Iron Company is a stock company, with a capital of $1,200,000, and has six furnaces. The size and capacity of each are as follows:

No. 1,	11 feet boshes,	47 feet high,	140 tons per week.
" 2,	13 " "	47 " "	150 " " "
" 3,	15 " "	47 " "	175 " " "
" 4,	18 " "	55 " "	250 " " "
" 5,	18 " "	55 " "	250 " " "
" 6,	16½ " "	60 " "	230 " " "

The hæmatite ore is obtained from Northampton, Lehigh, and Berks Counties, the magnetic from Lehigh Mountain, Pa., and Sussex and Morris Counties, New Jersey, and the limestone from the neighborhood. For the year 1872 this establishment consumed 108,274 tons of coal, 138,392 tons of iron ore, and 82,401 tons of limestone. Iron made during the year 54,037 tons. In connection with and for the use of the furnaces, there are car-shops, foundry and machine-shops, employing a large number of hands. Exclusive of miners, this company gives employment to about 1000 men.

The Catasauqua Manufacturing Company has a capital of $300,000. Its rolling-mill is engaged in manufacturing bar-iron, sheet-iron, and railroad-axles. It has a capacity of 13,000 tons per annum, and employs 350 men, using exclusively the pig-iron made in the Lehigh Valley. This company has recently bought out the Lehigh Manufacturing Company. In this branch of their works they employ 150 men, and make merchant bar-iron of various sizes. The ore for fettling the puddling furnaces is obtained from Port Henry, Lake Champlain, N.Y.

The amount of wages paid by the various manufacturing establishments in the borough averages $32,000 per month.

In the Catasauqua Car Works (Frederick & Co.) are made all kinds of cars, except passenger cars (coal, ore, freight, flats, etc.). They employ 130 men, and construct the whole of the car, except wheels and axles, having a foundry of their own, where castings of different descriptions are made. For the body of the cars, white oak exclusively is used, the lining being of white and yellow pine. In the foundry, nineteen tons of pig-iron are used per week, and twelve tons of forged iron. The capacity of the establishment is one hundred and fifty coal cars per month.

The Lehigh Car-Wheel and Axle Works employ 85 men, and consume from twenty to twenty-five tons of charcoal pig-iron a day. The capacity is 25,000 car-wheels per annum. Their iron comes mostly from Salisbury, Connecticut.

The Lehigh Fire-Brick Factory, owned by David Thomas (burnt in 1872, rebuilt same year), employs 40

C*

men and boys, and has a capacity of 2,000,000 bricks per annum, which are used in the Valley. The clay comes from New Jersey, and the sand from the neighborhood.

In addition, there are other smaller foundries and machine-shops, in which all manner of castings, steam-engines, etc. are made; also, a shovel-factory, where thirty-five different shovels, spades, and hoes are made; a factory of circular, cross-cut, and other kinds of saws; a saw-mill, with which is connected a planing-mill, sash and door factory, etc. Very large limestone quarries abound in this neighborhood, and are being extensively worked.

Of churches, there are 2 Presbyterian, 2 Roman Catholic (English and German), 1 Lutheran, 1 Methodist, 1 Evangelical, 1 Reformed. The Episcopalians, Free Methodist, and Welsh Baptists each have a mission here. There are two weekly papers published in the town. There is a national bank, with a capital of $500,000.

The Catasauqua and Fogelsville Railroad connects at Catasauqua with the Lehigh Valley Railroad. This road was built in 1856, and opened in 1857; it is twenty miles long, and has several branches. It cost $500,000, and was built by the Lehigh Crane Iron Company and the Thomas Iron Company, for the purpose of reaching the great iron-ore beds owned by these companies, the ore being now brought from the mines direct to the mouth of the furnaces. About four miles from Catasauqua, this road crosses the Jordan Creek on a splendid iron bridge, said to be one of the largest and handsomest in the country. It is 1100 feet in length, with 11 arches. Each truss is 16 feet high. The cost of the bridge was about $78,000.

Near the junction of the Catasauqua Creek and the Lehigh River, just above Catasauqua, stands an old and crumbling stone house, which is rendered of interesting importance by having once been the residence of George Taylor, one of the signers of the Declaration of Independence. The walls of the building are nearly two hundred years old, and when laid were very thick and strong. The house was frequently used as a place of refuge and defense against attacks of Indians.

HOKENDAUQUA.

This town is named from a small creek which empties into the Lehigh about half a mile north of it. It is an Indian name, and signifies *searching for land*, and was probably used by the aborigines in speaking to the surveyors or first settlers. It was laid out in 1855, and contains a population of 1200. The Thomas Iron Works are located here, consisting now of four furnaces, which are said to be the largest and to have the most powerful blast machinery in the United States, in which also their product of pig-iron is unexcelled. Two more furnaces are now building, and will soon be completed and in full operation. They are considered to be model furnaces, having all the valuable and recent improvements added to them. Their dimensions and capacity are as follows:

No. 1, 18 feet boshes,	60 feet high,	265 tons per week.
" 2, 18 " "	60 " "	265 " " "
" 3, 18 " "	55 " "	250 " " "
" 4, 18 " "	55 " "	250 " " "

There are five blast-engines, three of 1000 horse-power each, and two of 700 horse-power each. They are unusually beautiful specimens of workmanship. The fly-wheels are twenty-seven feet in diameter. They are also used for supplying the works and the town with water. The amount of coal consumed in the works is something over 100,000 tons per annum. The capital of the company is $1,750,000. In connection with the furnaces, there are here machine-shops, repair-shops, and car-shops. Altogether, 400 men are employed. The only church building here is one belonging to the Presbyterians. There are two furnaces at Alburtis, twenty-five miles west, on the Catasauqua and Fogelsville Railroad, which are owned and operated by the same company.

COPLAY.

This town (formerly Schreiber's) is named from a creek emptying into the Lehigh near Catasauqua, meaning, in the original Indian spelling (Copeechan), *a fine running stream*. It has been settled within a few years, and is the site of the Lehigh Valley Iron Works, which consist of three stacks of the following dimensions:

No. 1, 14 by 45 feet.
" 2, 16 by 53 "
" 3, 16 by 55 "

Their aggregate capacity is about 300 tons per week, and the number of men directly employed in them is 100. The extensive and valuable limestone quarries immediately adjoining seem almost inexhaustible. The capital of the company is $600,000.

The Coplay Cement Company, organized and chartered in 1866, capital $100,000. The mill is driven with steam-power, and contains one cracker and three sets of four-feet Esopus stone. There are in use four perpetual or draw kilns, thirty feet high and nine feet in diameter. The capacity of the works is 60,000 barrels per annum. In connection with the mill is an extensive cooper-shop. The number of men employed altogether is 50. The quarries are near the kilns, and contain a solid body of cement-stone, the thickness of whose stratum is as yet unknown. Its quality is thought by many to be superior to any in the market, recommendations to this effect having been frequently given.

WHITE HALL.

An outlet for business transacted by the railroad with the surrounding country. The name of White Hall Township was derived from the white-painted country-house of Lynford Lardner, Esq., of Philadelphia, which was a favorite resort of himself and friends, especially in the season when grouse abounded. The township, in 1763, was the scene of murderous attacks by the savage Indians. In this same township is the famous Egypt Church, the records of which date back as far as 1733. The first church was erected in 1742, being a small log building, with loose planks laid on logs for seats. The second church was built in 1785, and the third in 1851.

LAURY.

There are extensive slate quarries near by, and an old-established grist-mill. Large quantities of iron ore are also mined in the neighborhood for the furnaces along the river. The soil in this vicinity is very fertile, and the country unusually picturesque.

ROCKDALE.

This village is beautifully situated at the head of a pool of water, caused by the canal dam erected about a mile below, from which large quantities of excellent ice are annually shipped to Philadelphia. At this place great difficulty was experienced in the original construction of the road, owing to the barrier of slate-rock which abounded in such profusion. So steep and rugged were the hills that the engineers could not locate the road until the workmen had first gone through and cut paths with their picks and shovels. Even then they were obliged to be let down at points by means of ropes, at imminent risk to their lives. Parts of the cuts were at the height of 110 feet above the road-bed, and the cost of making the road in this section exceeded the rate of $100,000 per mile.

SLATINGTON.

This borough was laid out by the Lehigh Slate Company in 1851, although some quarrying had been done previous to this date. It has grown very rapidly in interest and importance, and is now the centre of a very extensive business in its specialty. The borough is divided by Trout Creek, which supplies fine water-power to the various establishments located on its banks. The population of the two settlements is about 2500, exclusive of Williamstown, distant about half of a mile. There is a Presbyterian church, and one used in common by the German Reformed and Lutheran congregations, also a Methodist Episcopal, and a Welsh Calvinistic Methodist. The Independent (Welsh) Evangelical congregation worship in the town-hall, and occasional services are held by the Episcopalians.

One weekly paper is published, and there is a Dime Savings Fund for deposit and discount.

The Lehigh Slate Company have extensive quarries, employing about 100 men, and having a capital of $100,000. They furnish school and mantel slate, having large factories in connection with their quarries.

The Franklin Quarries are about one mile from the borough, and employ about 80 men in getting out roofing slate.

The Girard Company manufacture roofing slate, and employ 80 men.

The Blue Mountain Slate Quarry is at Williamstown, and employs 60 men.

David Williams's Factory employs 50 men in the manufacture of school and roofing slates.

Besides these, there are the River-side Slate Co., the Blue Vein Company, the Star Slate Company, and other smaller establishments; having altogether, it is calculated, an aggregate capital of $500,000, and employing in all about 600 men.

It is the most extensive slate region in the country, and, it is thought, furnishes the finest quality of any, being of pure clay. The Capitol at Washington has been roofed with slates from these quarries, made expressly half an inch in thickness, and a number of shipments have been made to the regions of the Rocky Mountains.

During the year 1872, there were shipped by the different operators—

Of roofing slate	61,248 squares.
" school slate	11,047 cases.
" mantels and blackboards . .	3,747 "

In addition to which, there were sold at the quarries, and not shipped by railroad, 5754 squares, and of flagging 20,000 feet.

Some of the quarries may be seen on the left of the track, as we go north from the station.

From Slatington, a branch of the Lehigh Valley Railroad runs three and a half miles to Slatedale, where there are very extensive quarries and factories, employing 100 men, with a capital of $200,000.

In addition to the slate-factories at Slatington there is a foundry and machine-shop, where are made steam-

THE LEHIGH GAP.

Page 65.

engines, pumps, slate-sawing-machines, etc.; there are also a planing- and saw-mill, flour-mill, etc.

It is in contemplation to build a railroad to intersect the branch at Slatedale and run to Hamburg, Berks County, passing through an unusually rich farming country. Surveys have also been made and work commenced for an extension to this point of the Wilmington and Reading Railroad, which will form a direct southern outlet for coal, slate, and other products.

LEHIGH GAP.

Here the river Lehigh forces its way through the Kittatinny or Blue Mountains, which form the dividing line between Carbon County and Northampton and Lehigh Counties. The scenery at this point, but more especially as it is neared on either side, is sublime. It will well repay the traveler to stop off for a day and obtain the many picturesque views with which the neighborhood abounds. The craggy cliffs tower to a great height, and after scaling the mountains the tourist is amply compensated by the diversified and extensive prospect which the eye then commands, combining woodlands, and valleys, and mountains, and fields, in rare variety and beauty. On the western side is a lofty ridge, near the summit of which appears, emerging from the surrounding woods, a lonely pile of rocks, called "The Devil's Pulpit," upon which grow a few blasted pines. The shattered rocks thrown together in wild confusion, and the strata of rounded stones found hereabouts, have led some persons to suppose that the Lehigh, obstructed by the mountains, was formerly dammed up into a lake, which at length burst through what is now known as the Gap.

A factory is located here for the manufacture of mineral paint, the ore for which is found in the immediate neighborhood and is considered to be of excellent quality. The capacity of the works is about 500 tons per month.

KITTATINNY.

A brick-yard is situated here, having a capacity of 3,000,000 bricks per year.

PARRYVILLE.

This busy village is situated on the eastern bank of the Lehigh River, near its junction with the Poho Poco Creek, and is five miles south of Mauch Chunk, where much of the capital by which its business is conducted belongs. It was settled about the year 1786, and contains now 800 inhabitants. It contains 2 churches, Methodist Episcopal, and Evangelical.

The works of the Carbon Iron Company give to the place its business. The amount of its capital stock is $600,000, and there are three furnaces, employing 150 men. Their dimensions are as follows:

No. 1, 12 feet bosh, 52 feet high.
" 2, 15 " " 52 " "
" 3, 18 " " 65 " "

Their estimated capacity is 600 tons per week. The

hæmatite ore used in the furnaces is mined partly in the neighborhood and partly in Lehigh and Berks Counties. The magnetic ore is brought from near Dover, New Jersey, and the limestone from Northampton County.

A short distance below the village, on the west bank of the river, is a tract of fifteen or twenty acres, containing rocks of regular proportions and of blackest hue, for some time known as "The Devil's Garden," about which there are told some queer and quaint stories.

LEHIGHTON AND WEISSPORT.

These two boroughs are situated, the first on the western and the second on the eastern bank of the river, and are connected by a substantial wooden bridge, just above the junction of the Mahoning Creek with the Lehigh.

Lehighton was laid out some sixty years ago, by Col. Jacob Weiss and William Henry, the elevated piece of land upon which it is located giving an unusually favorable locality for a settlement. It contains about 1500 inhabitants, and, besides the usual number of hotels, stores, school-houses, etc., has two extensive tanneries, grist-mills, wagon- and carriage-, and furniture-factories, etc. The chief industrial establishment is the Stove Works, situated a short distance above the depot, employing on an average about 40 men. Although but recently put into operation, they have already built up a large and growing business. They make cooking-stoves chiefly, although other descriptions have also been successfully manufactured, all of them from their own designs and patterns, for some of which a good reputation seems acquired. In addition to their regular business, this company are also turning out considerable castings for sewing-machines, and a large amount of car-boxes.

The town contains a Methodist Episcopal church. Services are also held by the Presbyterians, Lutherans, and the Reformed Church.

Near the town is situated a mineral spring, the waters of which have proved very beneficial in several cases of disease and debility. It was discovered more than a century ago, and known then as "The Spring of the Healing Waters." As early as 1748 a petition was presented to the justices of Bucks County (of which this region was then a part) asking that a good wagon-road might be constructed from the King's road, near Bethlehem, to the Mahoning Creek, that persons might have easy access to this spring.

The grounds of the Carbon County Agricultural Society are located a short distance beyond, and are well supplied with the usual arrangements and accommodations for the annual fairs, the first of which was held in the fall of 1858. We would recommend to the traveler a drive through the Mahoning Valley near by, extending for fourteen miles, to Tamaqua. The scenery on either side of the mountains is of the most picturesque description, and sufficiently diversified to maintain one's interest throughout.

The history of this section of the county is peculiarly interesting. Here was situated the tract of land known among the fugitives from Wyoming as "The

Great Swamp," or "Shades of Death," afterwards called Towamensing, which is an Indian word, signifying *wilderness;* the only inhabitant of which at one time was a celebrated recluse, generally entitled "The Hermit of the Shades of Death," or "The Blue Mountain Hermit," the hero of at least one entertaining story.

The first settlement in the county was made by the Moravian missionaries, in the year 1746, at Gnadenhütten, near Lehighton, which became a most encouraging field, the Indian congregation alone numbering five hundred persons, the ministers being obliged to preach out-of-doors. The Rev. David Brainerd and the Rev. David Zeisberger were among those who labored here. Finally the settlement was removed to the north side of the river, and called New Gnadenhütten, the site of the present Weissport.

After Braddock's defeat, in 1755, the whole frontier was open to the inroads of the savage foe, and all the inhabitants lived in a state of constant terror. On the night of November 24th, 1755, the mission-house at Mahoning was attacked and burnt by a party of French Indians, and eleven of the settlers cruelly murdered. After the enemy had retired, the remains of the martyrs were gathered and interred. A plain slab in the old graveyard (within a short distance of the depot at Lehighton) marks the place, and bears a suitable inscription. A few years ago a small white marble monument was also erected to their memory by a citizen of Bethlehem.

As late as 1780, the Gilbert family, living in this neighborhood, were carried off into a bitterly painful captivity by a party of Indians, who took them to Canada and there separated them. At the time of its occurrence, this event caused intense excitement throughout the State, and several full and interesting accounts of it were written and published.

The Fort Allen Hotel in Weissport occupies the spot upon which the log fort was built by Benjamin Franklin, who was charged by the governor with the defense of the northwestern frontier. The well constructed by this famous printer, statesman, and warrior is still in a good state of preservation.

An extract from one of his letters to the governor reveals a curious state of morals then existing:

"We had for our chaplain a zealous Presbyterian minister, Mr. Beatty, who complained to me that the men did not generally attend his prayers and exhortations. When they enlisted, they were promised, besides their pay and provisions, a gill of rum a day, which was punctually served out to them, half in the morning and half in the evening. I said to Mr. Beatty, 'It is, perhaps, below the dignity of your profession to act as steward of the rum; but if you were to distribute only just after prayers, you would have them all about you.' He liked the thought, undertook the task, with the help of a few hands, to deal out the liquor, executed it to satisfaction, and never were prayers more generally or punctually attended. So I think this method preferable to the punishment inflicted by some military laws for non-attendance on divine service."

At Weissport, a rolling-mill is now again in active

operation, containing two heating furnaces and three double puddling furnaces, with a full complement of rolls and other machinery necessary to turn out thirty-five tons per day of merchant bar-iron, scrolls, band-iron, etc. The number of men employed is about 100. It is intended shortly to increase the capacity of the works, and to add punching- and spike-machines.

PACKERTON.

This busy town (formerly called Burlington) is named in honor of Judge Packer, the President of the Lehigh Valley Railroad. It is the forwarding office of the immense coal trade of the road, the numerous tracks laid here being used for making up the trains for their several destinations. The coal is also weighed here, for which purpose there are being constructed new and improved scales, 122½ feet in length, with a capacity of weighing 102 tons 16 cwt. in a single draught. Seven cars are usually weighed at a time, and while in rapid motion.

Here are located the most extensive shops of the Company (completed in 1863), whose chief work is that of building and repairing coal and freight cars. They are well supplied with the most improved modern machinery (to which additions are being made constantly), and are held in high repute. In their several departments there are employed about 560 men, requiring, on an average, $23,800 per month to pay their wages.

The dimensions of the principal buildings are as follows:

The main shop (a handsome structure of sandstone)	168 by 254 feet.
The machine-shop	85 by 41 "
The smith-shop	278 by 41 "
The iron-house	43 by 25 "
The oil-house	29 by 50 "
The paint-house	20 by 24 "
The store-room	16 by 20 "

During the year 1872, there were used of materials—

Cast-iron	2,953,600 pounds.
Wrought-iron	2,817,000 "
Cast-brass	112,104 "
Lumber	2,928,500 feet.
Coal	1,560 tons.

Near by is the extensive park (of which seventy-five acres are inclosed) belonging to the Lehigh Valley Railroad Company. Through its entire length there runs a beautiful stream, in which, as in several ponds at the eastern end, there are large quantities of brook-trout. It is also stocked with deer, elk, antelopes, etc.

At a distance of a mile and a half are situated the famous fish-ponds belonging to Lafayette Lentz, Esq., of Mauch Chunk, who is here largely engaged in the breeding of brook-trout, of which he has at times over 200,000. The arrangements for their propagation and cultivation are very complete, and the establishment has become an object of much interest to the many travelers in this neighborhood.

MAUCH CHUNK.

Mauch Chunk (Indian for *Bear Mountain*, and pronounced generally as though it were spelled Mauk or

MAUCH CHUNK AND MOUNT PISGAH.

Page 72.

Mawk Chunk), the seat of justice of Carbon County, was first settled about the year 1815. It was then a perfect wilderness, covered with forest-trees and undergrowth, and so completely hemmed in by high and steep mountains that it was as unlikely a spot as could be selected for a town, while any outlet by means of a wagon-road seemed wellnigh impossible.

As this wonderful town has been for so many years the centre of coal operations for the Lehigh region, it may not be inappropriate to condense a few of the leading facts concerning the first mining of coal in this valley. It was originally discovered by accident on the summit of Sharp Mountain (now the site of the town of Summit Hill), nine miles northwest of Mauch Chunk, in 1791, by a hunter named Philip Ginter, and is referred to in a communication to the State Historical Society, written by Dr. J. C. James, who traveled in this region in 1804. Having made known his discovery to Col. Jacob Weiss, residing at what is now known as Weissport, the latter took a specimen of it to Philadelphia and submitted it to the inspection of Messrs. John Nicholson, Michael Hillegas, and Charles Cist, who were so well satisfied as to its merits that, in 1792, they, with some others, formed themselves into what was called the Lehigh Coal Mine Company. Without charter or incorporation, they took up 8000 or 10,000 acres of unlocated land, including the Sharp Mountain. The company proceeded to open the mines, and made an appropriation of ten pounds ($26.67) to construct a road to the landing, a distance of nine miles. The mines were not worked to any extent, owing to the poor encouragement they received, until after the commencement of the war of 1812. They afterwards gave leases of their mines to different individuals in succession, the last of which was owned by Messrs. Cist, Miner, and Robinson, who started several arks of coal to Philadelphia, only three of which reached the city. They abandoned the business, disheartened by the public incredulity, in 1815.

The same discouraging results followed the attempted introduction of this fuel by the enterprising citizens of Luzerne County, where it is claimed to have been discovered by the Indians, and to have been known by the whites as early as 1768. People would neither purchase it (or, when they did, would afterwards complain of being imposed upon) nor take it as a gift. At the solicitation of Col. Weiss, an attempt was made, by permission of the Philadelphia city authorities, to burn it under the boilers at the Water-Works; but it was declared that it only served to put the fire out, and the remainder was therefore broken up and scattered on the sidewalks in place of gravel.

In the light of its present universal use, it is most amusing to recall the persistent discredit with which the public looked upon it in the beginning. Handbills were printed in English and German, stating the method of burning it, and including certificates from blacksmiths and others who had successfully used it. Sometimes journeymen were bribed to try the experiment fairly, so averse were they to any innovation of this kind. Luckily, charcoal became scarce and costly, and thus at length some were the more easily induced to test the new commodity; but it was many years before capitalists were led to put much faith in it as a profitable investment.

The expenses of hauling from the mines and of transportation to the city were very great, so that in the early experiments coal cost the shippers about fourteen dollars a ton when ready for sale in Philadelphia.

In July, 1818, the Lehigh Navigation Company, and in October of the same year the Lehigh Coal Company, were formed, which together were the foundation of the present Lehigh Coal and Navigation Company. The improvement of the Lehigh was commenced in August, 1818, and, under the skillful and energetic management of Messrs. Josiah White, Erskine Hazard, and George F. A. Hauto, the almost insuperable obstacles in the way of the river's navigation and the transportation of coal were at length overcome, and the success of the settlement assured.

The celebrity of the Lehigh coal is very extensive, from the fact that it is the hardest known anthracite in the world. The bed upon the top of Mauch Chunk Mountain is fifty-three feet in thickness, exceeding in this respect any layer or vein as yet discovered. In 1820, 385 tons completely stocked the market. Now, the shipments of the Lehigh Coal and Navigation Company alone reach sometimes as much as 18,000 tons per week.

With such constantly augmenting wealth, seeking shipment and general management at this point, Mauch Chunk, despite the natural difficulties in the way, has continued to grow and improve with remarkable rapidity. The town itself is built at the confluence of a creek with the same name and the Lehigh, and can now only enlarge itself by excavating sites from the precipitous rocks with which the narrow gorge abounds. About 200 feet above there is a level of several hundred acres, whereon stands a portion of the town called Upper Mauch Chunk. Back of this rises the majestic Mount Pisgah. This is the starting-point of the famous Switch-Back or Gravity Railway, which has been traveled with such rare gratification by tens of thousands. Until 1827 the coal was brought from the mines to the river in wagons. Mr. Josiah White (to whom this region must ever remain largely indebted for its development and prosperity) suggested and built this railroad. By means of stationary engines at the different planes, the empty cars are hauled up and returned to the mines, and the loaded ones brought as far as Summit Hill, whence they proceed by gravity to the shutes at Mauch Chunk. The grade varies from 50 to 90 feet per mile, except in the descent from Summit Hill to Panther Creek Valley, where it is 220 feet. The same unusual style of locomotion is also adopted for passenger cars, and affords a remarkable degree of amusement and enjoyment to the many visitors daily carried over this route. Recently a tunnel has been driven for about a mile through the Nesquehoning Mountain from the Panther Creek Valley; and it is the purpose of the company to ship its coal hereafter to Mauch Chunk by this route, retaining the Switch-Back road for passenger travel exclusively.

From the foot of Mount Pisgah a double track has been constructed with unusual care and strength to its summit, a distance of 2322 feet, with an elevation of about 900 feet above the river, at an angle of twenty degrees. The scene from the top of the plane is really sublime. The view of Mauch Chunk, Upper Mauch Chunk, East Mauch Chunk, nestling beneath the shadows of the mountains, with the Lehigh River winding its way at its base, and alive on either side with the steam-cars and canal-boats; the succession of mountain ridges, rising range after range; the distant view of the Lehigh Water Gap, with occasional glimpses of intervening fields and hamlets, and the much more distant view of Schooley's Mountains (sixty-four miles by rail); this and much more that cannot be described combine to make this panorama one of almost matchless beauty and grandeur; while the whole trip, with its novel and rapid method of transportation, the evidences of skillful engineering and mechanism, and the constant succession of charming landscapes, is fascinating and interesting in the extreme. It is thoroughly *unique*, and no one who has the opportunity of taking it should allow it to go by unimproved.

The railroad was finally put into operation in the year 1827 (May). At that time the only other railroads were those built from Baltimore to Ellicott's Mills, for which ground was broken July 4th, 1826, and at Quincy (Mass.), the latter being about three miles in length, and made in the fall of the same year. There had previously been a short wooden railroad (not plated with iron) at Leiper's stone quarry, about three-quarters of a mile in length; but this was worn out and not in use. Seven miles of this road to Summit Hill were laid out in the fall of 1818 and finished in 1819; and it is believed to have been the first road ever laid out by an instrument on the principle of dividing the whole descent into the whole distance, as regularly as the ground would permit, and to have no undulation.

On the east side of the river lies East Mauch Chunk, which, from the superior facilities for building, is growing more rapidly than either of the other two settlements. While it is a separate borough from Mauch Chunk proper and Upper Mauch Chunk, we have, for the sake of convenience, grouped the three under one head.

The town is very much resorted to during the summer and autumn months by lovers of pleasure and comfort. In every direction the scenery is most picturesque and entertaining, giving deservedly to the place the name of "The Switzerland of America." It is well supplied with gas, while few places enjoy so great and constant a supply of pure spring-water. It has two extensive iron-foundries and machine-shops for the manufacture of stationary engines, pumps, boilers, furnace, rolling-mill, mining machinery, etc. They employ about 150 men. There are also a steam flour- and grist-mill, car-repair-shops, several boat-yards, shoe-factories, sash- and blind-factory, etc. There is also a mill for the making of wire-rope, using annually about 500 tons of iron. The machinery for this branch of manufactures was first invented in Mauch Chunk. But for the limited room, many other establishments would long since have been founded. The shipping of the coal from the mines at Summit Hill, and the maintenance of the general offices of the two railroad companies, and of several collieries and other concerns, make it, notwithstanding, a place of great business and industry. There are two national banks, with an aggregate capital of $550,000, and one savings-bank. The population is about 6500.

A large addition has recently been made to the Mansion House, and it is now one of the most extensive and complete hotels in the state. It has rooms for 450 guests, and a dining-hall which will seat nearly 500 persons. It is fitted up with all the modern conveniences and comforts, and has already become a favorite resort for tourists and travellers. Its capacity is likely to be fully tested during the present year. Besides this house, there are several other large and well-kept hotels in the town.

There are three weekly newspapers published here, and churches belonging to the Episcopalians (a very beautiful stone building, recently erected at a cost of $70,000 upon a prominent and commanding site), Presbyterians, Methodists, Roman Catholics, Lutherans, and Evangelical Methodists; besides which there are Roman Catholic, Methodist, and Episcopal churches in East Mauch Chunk. In addition to the well-regulated free schools, there is a flourishing academy under the auspices of the Episcopal Church.

Mauch Chunk is the home of the Hon. Asa Packer, the President of the Lehigh Valley Railroad. His handsome residence, abounding with beautiful walks and terraces and gardens, made from a rugged and unpromising mountain-side, is an object that at once attracts the admiration of the stranger.

A handsome stone jail has lately been erected, upon a very complete model, at a cost of over $125,000.

There is a public library of over 1100 volumes, to which additions are being constantly made.

It is claimed that the first railroad-track ever laid down in the United States was in the street fronting the foundry of J. H. Salkeld & Co., for testing coal-car brakes.

It is believed that the first furnace in the country at which any considerable success was attained in the smelting of iron with anthracite coal (bituminous coal and coke having been hitherto used) was an old one at Mauch Chunk, temporarily fitted up for that purpose, in the fall and winter of the year 1837, by Messrs. Joseph Baughman, Julius Guiteau, and Henry High, of Reading.

An earlier attempt, however, was made in the use of anthracite for fuel in iron-manufacture, at Mauch Chunk also, in 1823 or 1824, in a furnace built especially for this purpose by some members of the Lehigh Coal and Navigation Company. It was several years after this date that similar experiments were tried at Kingston, Mass., and at Vizelle, on the borders of France and Switzerland.

Recently, various journals have had this whole matter under discussion, a number of articles and letters from parties engaged in this manufacture having been already published. As it is a subject of general interest, extracts from these documents are printed herewith in Appendix B, in which will also be found other important particulars concerning the iron trade.

At the Turnhole, a short distance above the town, formerly stood a famous bridge with a single span of 200 feet, the abutmeni on its north side being in this region an unexampled piece of substantial masonry. In 1857,

GLEN ONOKO.
(TERRACE FALLS.)

Page 81.

See Appendix D.

it was abandoned to avoid two very heavy curves (the hardest ones on the road), and a new iron double track bridge, with a very costly rock-cut at its north end, was completed, having two spans of 140 feet each.

GLEN ONOKO.

For full description of this beautiful glen, with additional illustrations, *see Appendix D.*

From Mauch Chunk to White Haven the scenery along the river is magnificently wild and picturesque. The dark waters of the Lehigh, dyed almost to a black by the sap of the hemlock pervading them, everywhere inclosed by mountains from 300 to 700 feet in height, and confined to a channel scarcely 300 feet wide, rush noisily and rapidly through a most circuitous route, perhaps the most irregular and rugged mountain region in the State. The curves are so constant and so abrupt, that there is a continual change of views, and some of the bends in the road describe nearly complete circles. In looking ahead, at times it seems almost impossible for the river to find its outlet. Hardly a spot of arable ground is to be seen, the hills sinking sheer to the water's edge, interspersed with cloves and gorges and tributary streams, and now and then with beautiful waterfalls, and spotted at intervals with tall, gaunt, and leafless trunks of withered pines. The geologist and botanist would feel himself amply repaid by a leisurely examination of the many forms of rocks and plants found here in luxurious abundance. Everywhere traces are to be seen of the devastating freshet of 1862, in the ruins of locks and dams and banks, comprising at one time the upper division of the canal of the Lehigh Coal and Navigation Company, but which has never been rebuilt north of Mauch Chunk.

BEAR CREEK.

The name of a wild torrent, upon which a saw-mill is located, and in whose waters the fisherman may be seen occasionally angling for trout.

PENN HAVEN JUNCTION.

At this point the Mahanoy, Beaver Meadow, and Hazleton Branches diverge from the main road, which, a short distance above, crosses to the east bank of the Lehigh. Passengers destined for places on any one of these several branches should be very careful *to change cars at this station.*

For description of the BEAVER MEADOW, HAZLETON, AND MAHANOY DIVISIONS, see pp. 125, 132, and 141.

STONY CREEK.

This is one of the most beautiful and romantic streams in the state, abounding throughout its whole length in scenery of the wildest grandeur, making a favorite locality for picnics. It is also much resorted to in the season by lovers of trout, large numbers of which are annually caught in its waters. The various saw-mills situated on the stream turn out a considerable quantity of lumber for shipment from this station.

DRAKE'S CREEK.

A shipping-place for lumber. A saw-mill is situated on the wild-brook that here enters the river through a deep rift in the hills. Near by, we pass through some

A VIEW ON STONY CREEK.

Page 82

abrupt cuts in the solid rock, so directly under the shadow of the mountains that we seem shut in from the rest of the world, amid ever-changing landscapes of charming scenery.

ROCKPORT.

This town is situated on the opposite side of the river from the station, in a very picturesque ravine. Before the freshet of 1862, it was the shipping-point of the Buck Mountain Coal Company, whose extensive mines are situated four miles distant. It was at that time considerably frequented during the summer season; but since the destruction of the canal, and the consequent removal of the Company's business, the place has assumed rather a desolate appearance.

MUD RUN AND HICKORY RUN.

These places are depots for the lumber trade of the two streams, which also furnish good sport to the fishermen. A few scattered houses contain the whole population, who find their employment in the saw-mills situated here.

TANNERY.

This thriving settlement was first made in 1855, about which time an extensive tannery (the second largest in the State) was established, the main building of which is 700 feet in length. Its capacity is over

50,000 hides a year, and it employs 70 men. Besides this establishment of I. M. Holcomb & Co., Shortz, Lewis & Co. and Dodge & Co. each have here large steam saw-mills, with a combined capacity of nearly 9,000,000 feet per annum. Albert Lewis's mill, on the opposite side of the river, has a capacity of 3,000,000 feet. There is no church building here, but services are maintained in the school-house and elsewhere by the Episcopalians, Methodists, and Presbyterians. Population, 600.

WHITE HAVEN.

This town was first settled in 1835, and named after Josiah White, the Superintendent of the Lehigh Coal and Navigation Company. It was incorporated as a borough in 1842. Until the freshet of 1862 entirely destroyed the canal, it was the head of slack-water navigation, and, as such, was a shipping-point of great activity. Soon after the completion of the canal, a packet-boat was run from White Haven to Mauch Chunk, and another from the latter place to Easton, which mode of traveling continued for several years, and, amid such scenery as then abounded along the whole route in even wilder grandeur than now exists, could not but have been greatly enjoyed.

Its principal business now is that connected with the lumber trade, of which it is the chief depot on the Lehigh. Immense quantities of logs and rafts may be seen at almost any time floating upon the surface of the ponds formed by two large dams across the river. On an average, in the spring, there are from twenty-five to thirty millions of feet of timber in the pool above the town.

The following list gives the names and production of the various saw-mills here, and of those at Bridgeport, about a mile below the town, also of two others in the immediate vicinity:

W. D. & E. F. Brown . .	40 men.	5,000,000	feet	per annum.
C. L. & A. S. Keck . .	30 "	4,000,000	"	"
Brown, Stoddard & Co. .	10 "	2,500,000	"	"
Werts, Stryker & Co. . .	10 "	2,500,000	"	"
A. F. Peters	18 "	4,000,000	"	"
Lehigh Grain and Lumber Co.	10 "	2,000,000	"	"
Davis, McMurtrie & Co. .	30 "	4,000,000	"	"
Keck, Childs & Co. . .	15 "	3,000,000	"	"
Jacob Stouffer . . .	10 "	2,000,000	"	"
Edwin Shortz . . .	16 "	3,500,000	"	"
Brown & Brader . . .	20 "	3,000,000	"	"

In addition to these establishments, Wallace & Breisch have a foundry and machine-shop, employing about 40 men in the manufacture of castings and saw-mill machinery. There are also three large ice-houses (one situated a short distance above the town), with a combined capacity of 30,000 tons.

The manner in which the town has recuperated under its several misfortunes is highly creditable to the pluck and real ability of its business men.

There are in the town churches belonging to the Methodists, Roman Catholics, Lutherans, Episcopalians, Presbyterians, and Free Methodists. There is a savings-bank, with a capital of $25,000. Population, 1500.

Passengers in going north dine, and in going south take supper, at the hotel immediately adjoining the depot, and may always be sure of a good meal.

The memorable flood of 1862, having obtained its first great impetus by the breaking of Dam No. 4, near White Haven, may properly be described under this heading. A heavy and continuous rain commenced on the afternoon of June 3d, 1862, and fell, with more or less intensity, until about one o'clock on the morning of the 5th. The Lehigh, swollen with its many tributary streams, and re-enforced by the giving way of dam after dam, with their vast accumulation of lumber and débris, soon became irresistible; and from White Haven to Easton its banks were the scene of total devastation. The water rose, it is computed, thirty feet above low-water mark, and with immense rapidity, —in some places as quickly as nine feet in five minutes. Every bridge across the river, as far as the Delaware (along whose shores also, for some distance below Easton, the effects of the freshet were disastrous), was totally carried away, except those at the Lehigh Gap, Bethlehem, and Easton.

Dwelling-houses and other buildings were swept off bodily, with all their inmates and contents, until they were safely grounded, or wrecked. The despairing cries of such as were thus, and in the canal-boats, hurried on to an inevitable death were most heart-rending. Very many were saved from destruction by the most wonderful escapes. The storminess and darkness of the night added immeasurably to the general alarm and gloom.

It has been estimated that there were at least one hundred and fifty lives lost, in addition to more than thirty million feet of lumber, one hundred and fifty canal-boats, etc. The loss in dollars and cents has been set down at $2,500,000. The destruction between Mauch Chunk and Allentown was so great that it involved the labor of between two and three thousand men and five hundred horses and mules for nearly four months before navigation was resumed. The railroads commenced running much sooner, although they sustained immense damage.

In Philadelphia and elsewhere, prompt and liberal subscriptions were made for the relief of the surviving sufferers, the funds being judiciously distributed by a committee selected from among gentlemen residing along the Lehigh.

MOOSEHEAD.

This station, formerly called Nescopec, is the location of the Moosehead Ochre Manufacturing Company. The raw material is found in the immediate neighborhood, and when prepared is used chiefly in the manufacture of oil-cloths. A short distance beyond White Haven, before reaching this station, we cross what is known as Cranberry Marsh, where the embankment originally made, soon after its completion, sunk sixty-five feet, pressing up the clay on either side. It is now substantially filled in, and no further difficulty has been encountered.

FAIRVIEW.

Here we are at the summit of the mountain, and cross the track of the Lehigh and Susquehanna Division of the New Jersey Central Railroad. A superb view stretches far southward, among mountains covered with oak and pine, uninhabited save by a few woodmen, and forming a vast wilderness.

NEWPORT.

From Fairview to Wilkes-Barre the distance, in a straight line, is a little less than five miles ; but we are obliged, in overcoming the mountain, to travel sixteen miles to reach the city, and at a grade of ninety feet to the mile. The view at this station is magnificent beyond description. The famous Wyoming (from Maughwauwame, the Indian name, signifying *large plain*) Valley, in all its romantic beauty, is here spread out in a broad panorama, containing in all about 40,000 acres. It lies along the banks of the Susquehanna (Indian for *broad, shallow river*), between two parallel ranges of mountains, extending from the northeast to the southwest and varying in height from 500 to 1900 feet. Some geologists have favored the theory that at one time this whole region was a vast lake, the Kittatinny Mountains, now serrated with gaps, forming a dam for the reception of the waters of the Chemung, Chenango, Delaware, and Susquehanna. While within these ranges all the land is underlaid with a greater or less number of coal-veins, outside of them none has as yet been discovered.

The geological structure of Wyoming affords to the scientific student a field of interesting investigation. The richness of the coal formation would arrest his

THE FIRST GLIMPSE OF THE WYOMING VALLEY.

Page 88.

attention particularly. On the top of the southern range of mountains the red shale, lined by the pebbly conglomerate (the bed on which the lower stratum of anthracite rests), with other accompanying rocks, is commonly observed. On the opposite mountain the same rocks appear, though less distinctly marked. Within the Valley nearly twenty strata of coal have been discovered, their thickness varying from four to twenty-eight feet. The quality of this mineral for purity is highly esteemed, several veins in an especial manner being excellent for the fusion of ores and the working of iron. During the war of the Revolution, several boat-loads were taken down the Susquehanna, it is supposed, by Captain Daniel Gore, for the use of the armory forges at Carlisle.

For twenty miles the silvery river may be seen meandering among the green meadows and fertile fields, entering the mountain-ridge which forms the north wall of this lovely valley through the Lackawannock Gap, a little north of Pittston, and leaving it again at the Nanticoke Gap, near Shickshinny. These mountains are very irregular in their formation, and are in general as wild as when discovered, being clothed with pines, dwarf oaks, and laurels, interspersed with other woods, deciduous and evergreen. The whole area is dotted here and there with towns, villages, and collieries, alive with the evidences of industry. To the south is Nanticoke. In front is Avondale, the scene of the terrible disaster in August, 1869, by which the lives of one hundred men and boys were lost and scores of families were made desolate, casting a heavy gloom over the entire country. A little north of this is the now largely-extended city of Wilkes-Barre. From its changed position, it is hard to believe that it is still the point which we are now aiming to reach; and yet the engineering skill by which the mountain is crossed is the theme of common admiration.

The history of the Valley abounds with narratives of adventure, excitement, and contest. In the earliest times, before its settlement by the white men, the Indians had fought many bloody battles for its possession. Like the Lackawanna, this valley early attracted emigrants from Connecticut, who believed it to be within the limits of the charter granted by the British crown to that colony. They endeavored to fortify their position still further by concluding a purchase of the territory from the Six Nations, who also claimed its ownership. There arose at once, owing in part to the imperfect knowledge of geography and surveying, a dispute between them and the people of Pennsylvania, who also claimed the territory as belonging to their original charter, which culminated in those fierce battles known as the Pennamite and Yankee wars, in which citizens on both sides, as well in their private capacity as through legislative action, were constantly embroiled. The dispute, after varying success, each party stoutly maintaining its rights, was finally referred to Congress, who appointed a committee to decide the question. This was done at Trenton, December 30th, 1782, giving to Pennsylvania the right of jurisdiction and pre-emption to the territory thus doubly claimed.

But this decree was differently interpreted, Pennsylvania holding that the Connecticut settlers could only obtain through her any legal title to the land which they claimed, while the Susquehanna Company of Connecticut, granting that jurisdiction was given to Pennsylvania, asserted that this did not affect the title by which they held the land. The animosity between the two parties was still at times very bitter, resulting in great embarrassments to the settlers, and not infrequently in personal and family feuds, the prejudices arising from which possessed the minds of subsequent generations. It was not until the passage of what was known as the Compromising Act of 1799 that this unhappy controversy was brought to an end. By this law it was provided that in seventeen townships, according to the survey of the Susquehanna Company, titles granted by that company, and occupied previous to the Trenton decree, should be considered valid on the occupant paying a small fee to the State, while the Pennsylvania claimant was to receive a certain compensation in case he released his claim to the Commonwealth. Commissioners were appointed under this act, who worked diligently for five years, until 1808, endeavoring to confirm the titles to the settlers and restore harmony between the contestants. The war of the Revolution put an end to their relentless strife for a time at least, since they saw the necessity of uniting against their common enemy.

The British, in 1778, had determined to make use of the Indians in this struggle, and accordingly induced a body of Iroquois to join a band of Tories under Colonel John Butler. Advancing to Wyoming, they easily captured Fort Wintermoot. The awe-stricken people now gathered from the surrounding country to a fort near the present site of Wilkes-Barre, called "Forty Fort" (after the forty New Englanders who built it), while three hundred and fifty men and boys, under Colonel Zebulon Butler, gallantly marched, on the 3d of July, to meet the enemy. The Americans fought bravely, and even gained ground, till Colonel Denison, wishing to take a more favorable position in the rear, bade his men fall back. This was mistaken for an order to retreat, and, amid uncontrollable confusion, they at last were compelled to yield before superior numbers. A general flight ensued, during which many were shot and tomahawked, while a few escaped to the fort. The prisoners were tortured with unheard-of cruelties, base treachery oftentimes luring them on to be most heartlessly murdered. Some twenty of them are said to have been ranged near a stone on the river-bank and held by savages, while Queen Esther, an old Seneca half-breed, walked round them in a circle singing their death-song and clubbing them until they died. (This s one is a conglomerate boulder, about eighteen inches high, and is still called Queen Esther's Rock.) It is computed that at least one hundred and twenty of the Connecticut people and from forty to eighty of the enemy lost their lives in this bloody engagement, while a still larger number are to be reckoned among the "missing."

The next day the fort was surrendered to the British leader on fair terms, with a distinct promise to protect its defenseless occupants; but no sooner were the savages admitted than they glutted their thirst for blood by putting to the most horrible deaths all they could secure. The rest sought safety in flight, but of these many died from exposure and fatigue, and a week later their dwellings were reduced to ashes. The fair fields of Wyoming presented a melancholy spectacle on the morning of the 4th; and from that time to the very end of the war there was hardly an hour's security for its inhabitants, who seemed to be the object of inextinguishable hatred on the part of their Indian and British assailants. In the course of this harassing warfare, there were many severe skirmishes, several heroic risings of prisoners upon their savage captors, and many hair-breadth escapes, some of which are minutely detailed in the records of those trying days.

It may amuse the reader to see a few lines descriptive of one of these escapes, written by a poet of the Revolutionary period:

"And many of the savage Indian crew
Did to the river's margin him pursue,—
But he before their frightful vengeance hied,
And plunged himself beneath the liquid tide,
And diving on his way, as he did flee,
Thereby to shun the savage enmity.
But while the buzzing bullets dashed around,
In his left shoulder he received a wound,
Which weakened him so much he thought it best,
When he approached the shore, awhile to rest.
When he had rested, he, with all his force,
Leap'd from the water and kept on his course;
When round the place a leaden shower did light
Which made the liquid billows foam with white:
Yet, notwithstanding these obstructions, he
Sprang up the bank, and got behind a tree.
When he his breath had gained, and was revived,
He urged his way, and at the fort arrived;
And there united with his friends again,
And thus escaped the brutal savage train."

To commemorate the sad events, more particularly the battle of July 3d (the harrowing details of which are well preserved in a number of histories), a monument was erected, in 1832, within the township of Wyoming, near the site where it was fought. It is a granite obelisk sixty-two and a half feet high, having upon marble slabs in front and on two sides appropriate inscriptions, recording the events of the massacre, and the names of the fallen, under the line of Horace:

"Dulce et decorum est pro patria mori."

It may be interesting to note here that it is thought that the famous Moravian nobleman, Count Zinzendorf, was the first white man that ever visited the Indian town of Wyoming, which he did on a religious mission.

Among the many points from which extensive views are had of the surrounding scenery, may be mentioned Bald Mountain, in Newton Township, about nine miles from Wilkes-Barre, which is 1750 feet high; Lee's Mountain, extending in a southeast direction, including Pulpit Rock, in Hollenback Township, and Honey Pot, its northeastern terminus, 865 feet high; Prospect Rock, 750 feet above the river, two miles from Wilkes-Barre; and Dial or Campbell's Rock, at the southwestern point of Capouse Mountain, and near Pittston. This rock, lying directly north and south, was the noon-mark of the first inhabitants of Wyoming, and hence it was called Dial Rock. Its other name is probably derived from the poet, Thomas Campbell, whose "Gertrude of Wyoming" has of itself so largely contributed to render this territory famous. All of these points, and a number more, are much resorted to by tourists and artists. The views to be obtained from them are of such rare beauty that, once seen, they can never be forgotten. So varied and extended is the prospect that one is truly lost in admiration of the magnificent panorama, and is instinctively led to adore the Almighty Creator.

WARRIOR RUN.

This station derives its name from a small creek running into the Susquehanna. Through the gap at this point it is said that the Gilbert family were taken to Canada after their capture by the Indians near Lehighton.

SUGAR NOTCH.

So called from the collieries formerly owned by Parrish and Thomas, which, with uniformly-painted breakers and dwellings, and the neat character of the latter, present altogether a much better appearance than the generality of such improvements.

These works now belong to the Wilkes-Barre Co l and Iron Company, and comprise two breakers, one slope, one shaft, and a tunnel 1500 feet in length, the longest in the Wyoming Valley. The combined capacity of the breakers is 1500 tons per day. When the new breaker, now in course of erection, is running, 1000 men and boys will find employment here. There is quite a succession of other collieries from this point to Wilkes-Barre, the particulars of which will be given in the description of that city.

SOUTH WILKES-BARRE.

This settlement having been incorporated within the city limits of Wilkes-Barre, its statistics will be included under that head.

WILKES-BARRE.

This is the oldest town in Luzerne County, having been laid out by Colonel John Durkee in 1772, at which time it embraced two hundred acres. It was incorporated as a borough in 1806. It derives its name from John Wilkes and Colonel Barre, distinguished advocates for liberty and the rights of the colonies. In 1772 there were but five white women in the town, and in 1784 the whole number of buildings was twenty-six, of which twenty-three were burnt by the Pennamites. The population for many years continued to grow steadily, but slowly. Within a few years past, it has increased more rapidly, until now, under the recent act, passed in 1871, whereby it was incorporated a city, with enlarged boundaries, it contains about 23,000 inhabitants. Its beautiful situation on the banks of the Susquehanna, and the excellent society abounding here, have always made it an attractive place to visitors.

Its early history is largely, and indeed mainly, connected with the wars between the Yankees and Pennamites, and between the colonists and the British and Indians, to which reference has already been fully made under the head of NEWPORT. It was within the township limits that most of the struggles for the possession of the Valley took place. Fort Wyoming is said to have stood on the river-bank, near Wyoming Street. Very few cities in America have records so full of interest and importance.

Its chief business is that connected with the mining and shipping of coal, of which there is great abundance in the immediate neighborhood.

The knowledge of the use of coal seems to have been communicated by the Indians to the whites, who, however, remained a long time incredulous concerning its value. In 1768, Charles Stewart surveyed the Manor of Sunbury, opposite Wilkes-Barre, and on the original draft is noted "stone-coal" as appearing in what is now called Ross Hill. In the year following, Obadiah Gore and his brother came from Connecticut with a body of settlers, and used anthracite coal in his blacksmith-shop. In 1766, Mr. Durham's boats were sent from below to Wyoming for coal, which was purchased from Mr. R. Geer, and mined from the opening recently the property of Mr. John W. Hollenback, above Mill Creek. We have already detailed the results following its discovery by Philip Ginther, under the heading of MAUCH CHUNK.

The use of anthracite for domestic purposes was discovered by the late Jesse Fell, for many years an associate judge of the county courts. We will give his own account of it, as recorded in one of the fly-leaves of his "Free Mason's Monitor."

"February 11th, of Masonry 5808. Made the experiment of burning the common stone-coal of the Valley, in a grate, in a common fireplace in my house, and find it will answer the purpose of fuel, making a clearer and better fire, at less expense, than burning wood in the common way. JESSE FELL.

"February 11, 1808."

News of this successful experiment soon spread through the town and country, and the old tavern of Judge Fell (corner of Washington and Northampton Streets) was visited constantly by persons anxious to witness the curious sight. Similar grates were soon constructed, and came into general use throughout the Valley.

From that time on, various efforts were made by different individuals to inaugurate in this region the coal trade, with what success the present wonderful prosperity and growth of this city and neighborhood plainly testify. In this connection, it may be interesting to republish the following letter, originally printed in *The Record of the Times*:

"SIR,—Having seen so much in various papers claiming the first mining of anthracite coal in Schuylkill County, in 1820, I beg leave to present the following facts, which date somewhat prior to the time claimed for our Schuylkill County neighbors.

"My father, Abijah Smith, came from Bridgeport, Connecticut, in 1806, and settled in the township of Plymouth. In 1807 he opened the Red Ash Coal Mine in said Plymouth. In 1808 he bought an ark of John P. Arndt, of Wilkes-Barre, ninety feet long and six feet wide, for thirty-five dollars. On November 9th of the same year (1808) he loaded it with coal twenty-four inches deep in the middle, and twenty-two in each end, making sixty tons of coal, gross weight, and ran it down the Susquehanna River to Columbia. He there had a blacksmith make a grate suitable for burning coal, and had it put in Gosler's Hotel. After having kindled his coal fire (which astonished the people), numbers came from miles away to see it, some coming from Philadelphia. From that time my father ran coal every season until his death, which occurred in 1826. In 1811–12, Abijah Smith & Co. sent coal to Havre de Grace, and there shipped it in schooners for New York City, consigned to Messrs. Prince & Waterbury, to sell on commission. In 1812 they sold about one hundred and fifty chaldrons (three hundred tons) at twenty-two dollars a chaldron (a chaldron contains about two tons). According to Messrs. Prince & Waterbury's account, rendered in 1812, they received $3692.20. Of this sum my father received only $762.12, after paying all expenses for getting the coal to New York. I presume he lost money by the operation.

"The above facts will, I think, correct the erroneous statement that the first coal was mined in 1820, in Schuylkill County. Yours truly,

"JOHN B. SMITH.

"PLYMOUTH, March 8, 1871."

According to Professor Rogers, the northern coal field extends in length fifty miles;—from Beach's mine, one mile below Shickshinny, to a point some distance above Carbondale,—and contains one hundred and seventy-seven square miles. The veins of coal vary in number from two to eight, according to location, and in thickness from one to twenty-eight feet. Taking the most reliable data we can obtain, it is estimated that this entire field contains about 2,285,600,000 tons of good merchantable coal, to which we may properly add 128,000,000 tons, the amount computed to belong to that portion of the eastern middle coal field lying in Luzerne County.

Wilkes-Barre being the centre of so much of the immense coal trade of the State, a few statistics of the companies having their headquarters here will prove interesting. Their works are situated in or near the city.

The Wilkes-Barre Coal and Iron Company (capital, $3,400,000) own thirteen breakers, one of which is abandoned for the present, a second is being enlarged, and two others will be at work in the course of a few weeks. The combined capacity of thirteen of them is estimated to be 1,608,000 tons *per annum*. The number of men and boys employed is 5000.

The Luzerne Coal and Iron Company are not yet fully at work, extensive and valuable improvements to the property being in progress. They have six collieries and shafts, and within two years expect to have them all in operation, when their combined *annual* capacity will be about 800,000 tons, and employment will be afforded to 2400 men and boys.

The Susquehanna Coal Company have, within seven miles of Wilkes-Barre, three breakers, with a combined *annual* capacity of 660,000 tons, the number of men and boys employed being 2300.

The Delaware and Hudson Canal Company mine

within two miles of the city about 2200 tons *per day*, and employ 1600 men and boys, working four breakers.

The Hillside Coal and Iron Company own four breakers, employing about 900 men and boys, and having a combined capacity of 2600 tons *per day*.

The Wilkes-Barre and Seneca Lake Colliery, one mile above the city, has one breaker, with a capacity of 400 tons *per day*, and employs 300 men and boys.

The Warrior Run Coal Company mine at one breaker 250 tons *per day*, and employ about 200 men and boys.

Hillman & Son employ about 140 men and boys, and mine about 200 tons *per day*.

Besides these coal operations, there are the establishments of the Vulcan Iron Works, for the manufacture of stationary engines, mine-cars, and other colliery work, employing about 100 men; the Dickson Manufacturing Company, employing 75 men, and the Wyoming Valley Manufacturing Company, employing about 35 men, both being engaged in the same work as above specified.

A large wire-rope-mill of the Hazard Manufacturing Company has recently gone into operation with a capacity of 1000 tons per annum. There are also saw- and planing-mills, carriage-factories, boat-yards, grist-mills, etc.

At different intervals between the years 1825 and 1851, several attempts were made to establish steamboat navigation on the Susquehanna. No less than six steamers, some of them of considerable size, were constructed at various places, and seemed for awhile to bid fair to become valuable additions to the trading and traveling facilities; but they were all compelled to be abandoned, the character of the river forbidding any hope of permanent success in this direction.

It was also imagined at an early day that large vessels could be built on its banks, and floated down, at the time of high water, to the seaboard. To test the matter, J. P. Arndt & Philip launched in 1803 a sloop of twelve tons' burden, named the "John Franklin," after that intrepid adherent of Yankee rights. She reached tide-water in safety, and high anticipations were immediately entertained of future success in this branch of business. A stock company was at once formed, town lots and timber lands advanced in price, and, amid the most sanguine expectations, the "Luzerne," a ship of between fifty and sixty tons, was launched in April, 1812. On her downward passage to the ocean she was dashed to pieces on the rocks at Conawaga Falls, near Middletown. With this catastrophe ended all attempts here at ship-building.

A short distance above the depot, the Lehigh Valley Railroad Company own a valuable tract of land four hundred feet wide and half a mile long, upon which a substantial brick round-house has been built, after the latest and best plans, with an iron truss-roof, having accommodations for thirteen engines. Extensive machine-shops, for general repairs mostly, are also in course of erection here, and will be fitted up with the most approved machinery.

The new county prison, erected recently at a cost of $200,000, is a very handsome and complete building, arranged with separate cells, after the manner of State prisons. The outside stone is from the vicinity of Campbell's Ledge, the inside stone from Meshoppen. The new court-house, erected about fifteen years ago, is an imposing edifice in the Romanesque style of architecture, costing about $85,000.

Among other public buildings may be mentioned Music Hall (a fine structure, accommodating thirteen hundred persons), Landmeser's Hall, and Liberty Hall, each holding five hundred. There is also a very neat and convenient market-house, owned by a stock company.

Among the many handsome private residences, the most costly and impressive are those situated on the river-side, which give to the already beautiful banks additional variety and attractiveness, and reflect great credit upon the taste and liberality of their builders.

There are the following churches: 3 Methodist, 4 Presbyterian, 3 Episcopal, 2 Roman Catholic, 1 Lutheran, 1 Welsh Presbyterian, 1 Baptist, 1 Reformed, 1 Welsh Congregational, 1 Jewish synagogue.

A commendable pride has always been felt by the citizens of Wilkes-Barre in their public schools, which are thought to be equal to any in the interior of the State. Several of the school-houses are constructed in the most approved manner, and will compare favorably with the best elsewhere. Altogether they will seat nearly two thousand pupils.

There is a Historical and Geological Society, with a valuable cabinet of curiosities, relics, and specimens. There is also a public library, with about one thousand volumes.

The Hollenback Cemetery is an old-established and beautiful cemetery. Ground near it has lately been purchased for a new cemetery for public use, to take the place of the former one, recently sold.

There are three national banks, with a combined capital of $850,000, in addition to which there are three savings-banks, with an authorized capital combined of $250,000. A large amount of capital is also in the hands of private bankers.

There are three street railways, running from the court-house to Ashley, Kingston, and South Wilkes-Barre.

Below the depot there has lately been erected a neat and substantial wire suspension bridge of seven spans, 658 feet in length. The cost of it was $32,000, subscribed by different parties to afford a safe crossing over the railroads and to aid in settling that part of the city.

By the Lehigh and Susquehanna Division of the Central Railroad of New Jersey, and by the Lackawanna and Bloomsburg Railroad passing through Kingston on the opposite side of the river, there is direct communication with Scranton on the east and Northumberland on the west, where connections are made with the great through-lines in various directions.

PLAINESVILLE.

Here is located the Enterprise Colliery, having one slope 950 feet, average of 20 degrees, one shaft, 145 feet, and one tunnel. The breaker has a capacity of 750 tons per day, and employment is given to about 250 men and boys.

PORT BLANCHARD.

Formerly the headquarters of raftsmen, who stopped here because of the good eddy. It is named after a family long residing here, and is opposite the town of

Wyoming, near "Queen Esther's Rock," of which mention has been made under the head of NEWPORT. It is the neighborhood of some of the operations of the Pennsylvania Coal Company, whose works are more fully described under the head of PITTSTON.

PITTSTON.

This busy town is situated at the point where the Susquehanna River and the North Branch Canal enter the great Wyoming Valley, and is well connected with railroads running in all directions. On the west rises the beautiful Lackawannock range of mountains.

It was formed in 1790, but prior to 1838 it contained only eight or ten dwellings. At this time Messrs. Butler & Mallery commenced operating in coal, since which period the town has rapidly advanced in prosperity. It was incorporated in 1853, and in the following year its boundaries were enlarged.

Within a radius of two and a half miles there is a population of 17,000, most of whom are more or less directly interested in the coal trade. The most extensive collieries are owned by the Pennsylvania Coal Company, whose total production for 1872 was 1,042,916 tons. The following statistics of their capacity, etc. may prove interesting:

There are in all twelve shafts producing coal, costing on an average $50,000 each. The average horsepower of each shaft-engine is 40; the average number of men and boys employed, 153. The average length of the gangways and breasts is two and a half miles.

There are 230 breasts in shafts working, the average length of which is 200 feet. The number of slopes outside is 4, of slopes inside, 4; of men employed at the outside ones, 100. The average horse-power of engine at each outside slope is 30, at each inside slope, 20. The number of breasts working in slopes is 62, the average length of which is 200 feet.

In addition, there are on the east side of the river many other collieries (more or less extensive), belonging to various parties, with a combined capital of something like a million and a quarter of dollars, and a capacity of 3500 tons per day.

Among the numerous mechanical and manufacturing establishments located here, may be mentioned steam grist-mills, breweries, wagon-factories, stove-works, extensive planing-mills, paper-mill, pottery, terra-cotta-works, tannery, car-repair-shops, steam bakery, etc., with the usual quota of tradesmen and storekeepers; the aggregate capital represented in these establishments, etc. being computed at $1,500,000.

There is one national bank, with a capital of $500,000, and two savings-banks, with a capital of $50,000 each. There are two weekly newspapers. There are churches belonging to the German Lutherans, German Reformed, Welsh Baptists, Episcopalians, Presbyterians, Methodists, and Roman Catholics. In addition to six public schools, there are several private seminaries.

West Pittston has a population of 1700. The town is beautifully situated on the west side of the Susquehanna, at the head of the valley, and, with its quiet and shady streets and picturesque views, furnishes a very attractive place of residence. A private seminary is situated here, and enjoys a moderate patronage. There are also two large public schools. An extensive foundry and machine-shop is located here, for the manufacture chiefly of stationary steam-engines and mine and mill-machinery. There is also the West Pittston Colliery, with a capital of $500,000, employing 150 men and boys, and with a capacity of 400 tons per day. On the 27th of April, 1871, a disastrous fire occurred in these works, whereby twenty miners lost their lives, leaving twelve widows and thirty-six orphans. The company is making a second opening, which will greatly increase their capacity. Davis and Park have also one breaker, with a capacity of 100 tons per day. The Methodists have a church-building here.

LACKAWANNA AND BLOOMSBURG JUNCTION.

The junction of the P. & N. Y. C. & R. R. Company with the Lackawanna and Bloomsburg Railroad for Scranton in the north, and Shickshinny, Berwick, Bloomsburg, Catawissa, Danville, and Northumberland in the south and west.

A short distance above, the Pleasant Valley Branch of the P. & N. Y. C. & R. R. Company connects the main line with a number of valuable collieries.

COXTON.

One mile above the L. & B. Junction, and opposite Campbell's Ledge,—from which, as already noted, a superb view may be had of the Wyoming Valley. Many travelers pronounce it the finest of all, it having this advantage, that the two mountain-ranges which inclose the valley are both seen at once, and the whole valley is given in greater completeness than from any other point. Here are located the weigh-scales and forwarding offices of the P. & N. Y. C. & R. R. Company, an engine-house, turn-table, side tracks for the making up of trains, etc., answering in this upper section of the road to Packerton below.

It is named in honor of Mr. John P. Cox, who at the time of his decease was the Superintendent of the P. & N. Y. C. & R. R. Co. Near by is a beautiful water-fall known as the Falling Spring.

RANSOM.

A depot for Ransom and Exeter Townships, the latter of which is on the opposite side of the river, where there is a large flouring-mill.

FALLS.

So called from a handsome cascade on Buttermilk Creek within sight of the railroad. Depot for Falls Township, accommodating also quite a portion of Susquehanna County. It contains flouring- and saw-mills, keg-factories, etc.

McKUNE'S.

Depot for Keelersville (on the opposite side of the river) and other portions of Wyoming County.

LA GRANGE.

Contains flour- and saw-mills, and is the home of the Osterhaus family, for many years residents of this section.

TUNKHANNOCK.

An Indian name for the smaller of two contiguous streams (Bowman's Creek and Tunkhannock), now, however, applied only to the one. It is the county town of Wyoming, and since the completion of the railroad it has become an important business centre. It was settled in the early part of the century, and now has a population of about 1200. It contains a large tannery, saw- and grist-mills, iron-foundry, furniture- and sash-factories, planing-mills, etc., also Presbyterian, Methodist, and Baptist churches. An Episcopal church is about to be erected. There is also a Masonic hall. A national bank is located here, with a capital of $100,000, besides which there is a private banking-house. The town (which is very picturesquely situated, and altogether very prepossessing in its appearance) is supplied with fine water from the mountain springs. There is in construction from this point a narrow-gauge (three feet) railroad to Montrose, twenty-seven miles distant (the county town of Susquehanna), passing through Springville also, a former residence of the Hon. Asa Packer. It is now finished as far as Hunter's, and the whole road is expected to be open for traffic by the end of the present year.

VOSBURG.

The depot for Washington Township. The ride hence to Mehoopany reminds one of the famous Ox-bow on the Lehigh. From one town to the other, it is one mile in a straight line; by rail it is seven miles. The scenery along the road on either side of the river is most beautiful, abounding in the richest variety.

MEHOOPANY.

The town, which is upon the opposite side of the river, derives its name from the creek near by. It contains Baptist and Methodist churches, plaster-, flour-, and saw-mills, and is quite a depot for lumber. A large tannery is also in course of erection. On the sources of this creek is found the first bituminous coal after leaving the Wyoming Valley. Iron ore is also to be had here. As early as 1832, quite an excitement was created by reported discoveries of deposits of copper on the creek, from which, however, no advantage has been known to follow.

MESHOPPEN.

So named from the creek upon which it is situated, and which rises in the neighborhood of Montrose. It was settled about 1820, and contains a population of several hundred. Besides Methodist, Presbyterian, and Universalist churches, the town contains a tannery, grist-, saw-, and plaster-mills, marble-yards, etc. Its chief business, and one becoming quite extensive now, is in the quarrying of a valuable limestone, found hereabouts in abundance, used for curbs, flagging, steps, etc., and very much admired wherever put down.

BLACK WALNUT.

Depot for Brintrim Township. There are large quarries here of the same blue-stone as is found at Meshoppen below, which are being rapidly developed.

SKINNER'S EDDY.

Situated upon the two Tuscaroras. Formerly one of the finest and most important harbors and landings on the river. Frequently, when the descending navigation of the Susquehanna was the only way of reaching the market, there have been here over-night hundreds of rafts and arks. It contains a Methodist church. Still another quarry of blue-stone is being worked here to advantage.

LACEYVILLE.

So called from an old resident named Lacey. Settled about 1830. Population, about 300. It contains a Baptist church, grist- and saw-mills, and an iron-foundry, where agricultural implements, etc. are made. The stone quarries here are of excellent quality for pavements, sills, lintels, platforms, etc. One stone was taken out lately that measured sixteen feet square.

WYALUSING.

This town, which derives its name from the creek emptying here into the Susquehanna (although it was called by the natives M'chwihilusing, meaning *beautiful hunting-ground*, or, as others say, *the home of the great patriarch*), has a remarkably interesting history. The creek meets the river here in one of those fine intervales which characterize the scenery of the Susquehanna, and at the junction of the two valleys there is a considerable scope of slightly rolling land, spoken of by the early travelers as the "Plains of Wyalusing." It is believed that the Lenni-Lenape or Delaware Indians for many years occupied the valley as far as Tioga, the south door of the Iroquois or confederated Five Nations, from which they were expelled by the latter after a long series of bloody battles. The great war-path leading southward extended as far as Shamokin, the present site of Sunbury, which for many years continued to be a place of general rendezvous for the war and hunting-parties of the Iroquois and their allies. Wyalusing, being about a day's journey on this highway from Tioga, afforded a convenient halting-place. After the white people began to purchase territory of the Iroquois and their confederates, the Susquehanna Valley, below Tioga, was reserved as a general asylum for the Indians who became dispossessed of their lands.

Which of the several clans located hereabouts occupied the village of Wyalusing when it was first visited by the Moravian missionaries, cannot be definitely settled; but most likely it was the Delawares. Among them, in the middle of the last century, a remarkable desire for the gospel was awakened. In 1762, Papunhank, a false prophet, who had obtained some knowledge of Christianity, preached to them a sort of heathen morality. In this, however, they soon lost faith, and, desiring some better religious teachers, David Zeisberger, the great Moravian apostle to the Indians, and a Delaware convert named Anthony, responded to the call. He was subsequently appointed resident missionary by the Brethren at Bethlehem. His labors were unusually successful. He baptized Papunhank, and there were good hopes of converting the whole clan, but Pontiac's war breaking out at this time, the mission was held in abeyance for three years. At the conclusion of peace, Zeisberger led the remnants of Christian Indians from Philadelphia back to the Susquehanna, and began to found a Christian town near the site of the heathen village, giving to it the name of Friedenshütten, or *tents of peace.* In 1767 a large and convenient church was erected, with a cupola and bell, the first that ever sounded over the waters of the North Susquehanna.

For fear of becoming involved in the impending strife, and to remove themselves from the demoralizing influences of traders and other bad men, the Christian Indians, in June, 1772, emigrated to Ohio to the number of over two hundred persons.

To commemorate these missionary labors, and mark the site of the village, members of the Moravian Historical Society, at Bethlehem, erected in June, 1871, with appropriate and impressive ceremonies and services, a handsome stone monument engraved with suitable inscriptions, which may be seen just before reaching the depot from the south.

The town contains a wagon-factory, flouring- and planing-mills, and churches belonging to the Presbyterians, Methodists, and Baptists. Population, 500. Upon the creek there are several mills and factories, giving employment to a considerable number of hands.

FRENCHTOWN.

This is the depot for the township of Asylum, so called from the settlement here of French refugees who fled from Paris at the time of the Revolution at the close of the last century. Among them were Viscount de Noailles, Omar Talon, and others who were connected with the royal household, and who, upon landing in Philadelphia, met with Robert Morris and John Nicholson. These gentlemen owned large tracts of uncultivated land in Pennsylvania, and with them the refugees formed an association known as the Asylum and Holland Land Company, and increased their estates to a million of acres. Although with a liberal expenditure of money and industry the wilderness was soon converted into an attractive settlement, yet the colony lasted for only a few years, they gladly accepting the offer of returning to France in peace. They left most of their improvements in the possession of two or three remaining families, whose descendants are among the best farmers of this region.

Louis Philippe (at that time Duke of Orleans), it is said, spent a winter here with his faithful adherents. It was believed that arrangements were in progress to have the king and queen make their escape from France and hide themselves in this asylum. Certain it is that a house was built far back in the woods, and called the Queen's House.

The town contains flouring- and saw-mills.

RUMMERFIELD.

Depot for the inhabitants living upon the creek from which the station derives its name.

STANDING STONE.

So called by the Indians because of a stone standing in the river opposite the village, which no doubt has fallen from the hills, although it differs somewhat in formation from those that skirt the river. It is erect and stationary, measuring forty feet in and out of the water. Rumor has it that one corner of it was shot off by General Sullivan in his tour through this country.

WYSAUKING.

So called from the creek near by, whose Indian name signifies *the place of grapes*. It was settled in the last century, and is an important depot for the adjoining villages and townships. It is the residence of Colonel Victor E. Piollet, whose estate, consisting of over twelve hundred acres, is celebrated as one of the model farms of the State.

TOWANDA.

This thriving town (the capital of Bradford County) is beautifully situated on the west bank of the Susquehanna, and surrounded with scenery of a very picturesque description. It was settled in 1812, and incorporated in 1828. It was laid out by Mr. Means, after whom it was at first called Meansville, and subsequently Williamston. At length it obtained its present name from the creek emptying southeast of the town, the original form of the Indian word being Tawandee, or Awandee, meaning, *at the burial-place*. It has been thought by some to be the same name as Gowanda, meaning *a town among the hills by the water-side*. The Nanticoks are supposed to have buried the bones of their dead there.

The Pennsylvania and New York Canal and Railroad Company's road intersects here the Barclay Railroad and the Sullivan and Erie Railroad, which are used chiefly for the transportation of the bituminous coal found in the neighborhood. It has also under its control the North Branch Canal. Towanda has thus become a point of considerable importance in the shipment of coal. In 1872 the Towanda Coal Company mined 257,766 tons of bituminous coal, the Fall Creek Company 100,013 tons, and the Sullivan Anthracite Coal Company 54,966 tons.

Among the mechanical and industrial establishments may be mentioned the following: the shops of the Towanda Coal Company, for making and repairing coal cars, steam planing-mills, sash- and blind-factories, house-furniture manufactory, the Towanda Agricultural Works, a steam grist-mill, wagon- and carriage-factories, machine-shops for steam-engines, grist- and saw-mill irons, castings, etc., boot- and shoe-factories (one of which employs nearly 100 hands), the Towanda Iron Manufacturing Co.'s rolling-mill (capital, $55,000) for cut spikes and nails, the Towanda Eureka Mower Company, with a capital of $100,000, etc.

In addition to these branches of business, there is a very large trade done in country produce (a rich agricultural section being in the rear), dry-goods, etc. Immense quantities of poultry and butter are annually shipped to many and distant places. One store, employing sixteen clerks, has sold as much as $350,000 worth of dry-goods and provisions in the course of a year. The Schraeder Mining and Manufacturing Company, lately organized, with a capital of $300,000, have already commenced operations, and expect to have their railroad connections made in time to ship 50,000 tons of coal during the present year.

There is one national bank, with a capital of $125,000, and there are also several private banking-houses. There are three weekly newspapers, and churches belonging to the Roman Catholics, Presbyterians, Episcopalians, Methodists, Baptists, and African Methodists. Besides the public schools, there is the Susquehanna Collegiate Institute, designed for both sexes. It is under the auspices of the Presbytery of Lackawanna, is eligibly situated, and commands a large patronage. The number of pupils for the year 1871–72 was 229, about evenly divided, of whom about 30 were boarders.

The town has a population of 4000. In addition to the court-house, there are halls belonging to the Free Masons, Odd - Fellows, and other parties, and also Mercur's Hall, capable of seating 500.

The bridge of the Lehigh Valley Railroad, crossing at the upper part of the town, is a fine structure of wood and iron, consisting of nine spans, resting upon two abutments and eight stone piers, the total length being nearly 1500 feet.

ULSTER.

Depot for Sheshequin (a name given to the greater part of this immediate valley) and Smithfield Townships. Contains planing-, grist-, and saw-mills; also a Methodist church. The original name of the town itself was Sheshequin, the name now given to the settlement on the opposite side of the river. It was for a number of years a mission station of the Moravians.

MILAN.

A small settlement, containing a saw-mill and stores, with ordinary country trade.

In the immediate neighborhood, extending north and south for several miles, are situated what have for years been known as "Queen Esther's Flats," called after the famous Indian queen of this name. Her history is one of remarkable interest. Some have thought her to be the same as Catharine Montour, who is said to have been a half-breed daughter of one of the French governors of Canada, where she received her education. Others have made her to be a sister of Catharine Montour. Her village, said to have contained about seventy houses of rude form, was located about a mile below Athens. Near by stood her "castle," where she held stately court. She married Tom Hill, an Indian as forbidding as herself, and, after she left Tioga, went to Onondaga to reside.

ATHENS.

This interesting town is situated in a beautiful portion of country, at the confluence of the Susquehanna and Chemung (meaning *big horn*) Rivers. This spot was known during the Revolution, and in the early part of this century, as Tioga Point. Tioga (meaning *the meeting of the waters*) is still the legal name of the river, legally known in New York as the Chemung. Prior to the Revolution, and as far back as 1737, when Conrad Weiser, a celebrated interpreter and Indian agent for the government, made his first visit to the Six Nations, it was the site of the Indian town Diahoga, the most extensive Indian settlement within the jurisdiction of Pennsylvania, north of Shamokin, it being on the main trail of the Six Nations from the Wyoming Valley to the Lakes. It was the "south door" of the "Long House" of the Six Nations, and was guarded by the Senecas. After the Six Nations conquered the Delawares, they brought them up to Diahoga to live, and this, until the year 1758, was the principal seat of that tribe. The chief man then among them was Tee-dy-us-cung, who styled himself "King of the Delawares," and who, nearly every year, went down to Philadelphia with a large retinue of warriors, women, and children, and held treaties with the governor, returning to the seat of his kingdom laden with presents. During the French and Indian wars, Teedyuscung and his nation were disposed to be friendly to the English, and in 1758 they removed to Wyoming, in order to be under the protection of the government, where the governor caused houses to be erected for them. After the departure of the Delawares, Diahoga was, for some years, occupied or inhabited only as a summer residence or hunting-ground by the Six Nations.

It was at this place, then becoming known as "Tioga" and "Tioga Point," that Butler, and perhaps Brant, with their English and Indians, rendezvoused and prepared for their descent on Wyoming, and hither they returned after the battle.

In September, 1778, Colonel Hartley, with a force of 400 men, ascended the river as far as this place, and burned Tioga, with Queen Esther's palace and town. In the following year, during his expedition against the Indians, General Sullivan made Tioga the base of his operations. He arrived here from Wyoming with 3500 men on the 11th of August, and erected a stockade, extending across the peninsula from river to river, called Fort Sullivan. General Clinton pushed across the country, from Albany to Otsego Lake, with 1800 men, and floated down the river, uniting his forces with Sullivan August 22d. The whole army lay here until the 27th, when it went on its march of devastation, leaving Tioga a military station, under command of

Colonel Shrieve, whence Sullivan derived his supplies, and to which he sent his wounded. The expedition returned here victorious, and on the 4th of October the fort was demolished, and the army went down the river to Wyoming. About 1783, white adventurers and pioneers first crept up the river as far as Tioga Point. The first of whom there is any positive information was a man named Patterson, who *squatted* on the east side of the Susquehanna, as did shortly after one Miller and one Moore. About 1783, a Dutchman named Budd erected a cabin on the Point, and in the next year Jacob Snell settled west of the Tioga, where, on the 5th of July, 1784, was born the first white native,—the late Major Abraham Snell.

In 1784, or early in 1785, Matthias Hollenback opened here a trading-house: among his early clerks was John Shepard, then a young man, who remained here, and afterwards became quite an extensive land-holder. In May, 1786, the Connecticut Susquehanna Company issued a grant for a township, to be called Athens, and in May and June of that year it was surveyed and laid out by Colonel John Jenkins, Colonel John Franklin, and Colonel Elisha Satterlee. Colonel Satterlee and his brother-in-law, Major Elisha Mathewson, came up from Wyoming and made improvements in 1787; the next year they settled here permanently. Colonel Franklin built a house here in 1787, and was intending to settle here the same year, but was arrested for high treason against the State of Pennsylvania, and confined in irons in Philadelphia. It was alleged that the Connecticut settlers, of whom he was the recognized leader, were about to erect a new State in Northern Pennsylvania, with Franklin as governor. He was detained in prison nearly two years, and immediately after his release, in 1789, settled in Athens. Franklin, Satterlee, and Mathewson were the most prominent of the early settlers; they had all served in the war, were in Wyoming during the troubles, and had been here with General Sullivan.

To the northwest of the town is Spanish Hill, one of the curiosities of this section. It is a bluff, rising from the centre of the valley to a height of about 175 feet, and commanding a charming view for many miles around. Remains of ancient fortifications around the summit of the hill have been seen by many of the present generation. Some of the early settlers have been heard to say that the Indians called it Spanish Hill, implying that the Spaniards had been there. Hence also the rumors that Spanish coins had been found there. The Indians seldom went on the hill, from some superstitious dread, it having the name of being a particularly fatal place to their nation.

Athens was incorporated in 1831 as a borough, and has a population of about 1000. It contains Baptist, Methodist, Universalist, Episcopal, Presbyterian, and Roman Catholic churches, and supports two weekly newspapers. There is a national bank situated here, with a capital of $100,000. The principal business establishments are the Steam Agricultural Iron Works of Blood & Co., employing about 40 men; Underhill's Tannery, employing about the same number of hands, and with a capacity of 25,000 hides per annum; and Kellogg's Bridge Shop, whose work is now extending into various distant regions. A large and increasing trade is done in butter, hay, and grain. Besides the graded public schools, there is one private academy.

SAYRE.

For particulars of this important new station, see Appendix E.

WAVERLY.

This important and flourishing town is properly the northern terminus of the Lehigh Valley Railroad, which here makes direct connection with the Erie Railway for Elmira, Watkins' Glen, Rochester, Buffalo, Niagara Falls, Detroit, and all points west and northwest. It is very eligibly situated on a commanding and serviceable tract of land, with the Chemung River on the west, the Susquehanna on the east, and the Cayuta Creek (with large water privileges) running in the centre. It is embraced within a purchase of a thousand acres (at five dollars each), made in 1796 by Mr. John Shepard, of General Thomas, of Westchester County, New York. The tract at this time was a perfect wilderness, and the improvements were very gradual until 1848, when the Erie Railway reached this point. From that time its growth has been rapid and substantial.

It was incorporated as a borough in 1854. In June, 1871, a very disastrous fire occurred, causing a loss amounting to $100,000; and yet, as in many other towns, what seemed a great calamity was converted into a public benefit, a much better class of buildings taking the places of those destroyed. In addition to the railroad connections already named, and a short distance below, with the Ithaca and Athens and Southern Central Railroads, the Pennsylvania and Sodus Bay Railroad to Lake Ontario is also now building to this point. It is one of the largest butter and grain depots on the Erie Railway, whose freight receipts here (largely on account of transfers) are in excess of those of several other considerable towns on the road combined. Among the numerous manufacturing establishments may be mentioned a paper-mill (employing 20 hands), woolen-factory (20 hands), tanneries, grist- and planing-mills, sash- and blind-factories, foundry (for agricultural implements chiefly), carriage-factory, etc. Gas-works are to be put into operation by the 1st of October, and a large and handsome hotel, to cost $60,000, is nearly finished. The opera-house, one of the finest edifices of the kind in the State, was opened in February, 1871, and destroyed by fire in February, 1873.

The public schools are well graded, and furnish an excellent education to the pupils attending them. There are churches belonging to the Roman Catholics, Baptists, Episcopalians, and Methodists. Services are also maintained by the Universalists. Two weekly papers are published here. There are two national banks, with a combined capital of $156,100.

Population, 5000, including Factoryville and Milltown, which lie immediately contiguous. A short distance below the town, the P. & N. Y. C. & R. R. Company have erected pockets for transhipping coal to the Erie Railway, where about 2000 tons can be handled per day.

The improvements now being made on "The

Plains"—a valuable addition to the town—are fully described under the head of SAYRE. This whole neighborhood is fast becoming a busy railroad and manufacturing centre.

BEAVER MEADOW DIVISION.

PENN HAVEN.

This streetless village was first commenced in 1838, when it was selected by the Hazleton Coal Company (now merged with the Lehigh Valley Railroad) as their shipping-point, from which a large business was done, although it was seriously interrupted by the destructive freshet of 1841. From 1838 to 1852, the company used the Beaver Meadow Railroad, and after the freshet of 1850, they located and built the present branch road from Hazle Creek Bridge to the top of the mountain at Penn Haven, whence, by means of self-acting inclined planes (430 feet high and 1200 feet long), the coal is now shipped directly to market.

BLACK CREEK JUNCTION.

The point at which the Beaver Meadow and Hazleton Divisions meet the Mahanoy Division.

WEATHERLY.

This town (originally called Black Creek) derives its present name from David Weatherly, a clockmaker of Philadelphia, one of the original directors of the Beaver Meadow Railroad and Mining Company.

In the place of the shops formerly owned by the Beaver Meadow Railroad Company, and which (together with nearly one-half of the superstructure and a large portion of the permanent roadway towards Penn Haven) were destroyed in the great freshet of 1849–50, the Lehigh Valley Railroad Company have erected here large and substantial works. They afford employment directly to about 170 men, and give to the town quite a busy aspect. The entire establishment forms a hollow square, and was commenced in the spring of 1867, and completed in January, 1869, and is well supplied with the most approved machinery. The following are the dimensions of the principal buildings:

Machine-shop	150 by 112 feet.
Carpenter-shop	85 by 42 "
Moulding-room	150 by 52 "
Smith-shop	85 by 42 "

The round-house has accommodations for sixteen engines.

During the year 1872, the manufactures in the foundry were as follows:

Iron castings, 2,874,822 lbs.; brass, 209,980 lbs., Babbitt's metal, 1493 lbs., and spelter for telegraph batteries, 683. 716 tons of pig-iron were consumed, besides 1,156,170 lbs. of scrap iron; 37,895 lbs. of brass; 6835 lbs. of copper; 111,542 lbs. of scrap brass; and 9270 lbs. of tin. Some of the finest locomotives on the road have been constructed here, in addition to which coal cars are made and repaired, and iron-work for bridges, brass and iron castings, etc. Nearly all the castings used at the Packerton and Delano shops, and on the Mahanoy, Beaver Meadow, and Wyoming Divisions, are made here. During the year 1872, three new locomotives (the most powerful now employed in coal transportation) were built, and thirty-eight old ones repaired.

There are churches owned by the Presbyterians and Methodists, and a public hall used by various societies. The population of the town is about 1500.

Immediately above Weatherly, the road is built for a distance of nearly two miles at the remarkable grade of 145 feet per mile, and 135 feet per mile for some 4000 feet farther.

HAZLE CREEK BRIDGE.

The junction of the Beaver Meadow and Hazleton Divisions and of the Buck Mountain Branch. The works of the Buck Mountain Coal Company are situated three miles to the north, and consist of two slopes and one breaker, with a capacity of 3600 tons per week, employing 300 men and boys.

BEAVER MEADOW.

This town (pleasantly situated on elevated ground, 1600 feet above tide-water) was first settled about 1833, although at that time the original house, built in 1804, was still standing. It derives its name from Beaver Creek (running near by), upon which a dam is said to have existed, built by the beavers.

In 1806, the Susquehanna and Lehigh Turnpike, running from the Nesquehoning Creek and above to the Susquehanna, was completed and opened to the public.

Coal was taken away from Beaver Meadow as early as 1812, being conveyed to Berwick and Bloomsburg, where it was used in blacksmithing. Subsequently to 1826, it was also hauled to the Landing Tavern (just above Mauch Chunk), and sent thence by arks to Philadelphia, and sold at eight dollars per ton.

The Beaver Meadow Railroad and Mining Company was incorporated in 1830, and built the first road from its mines to Parryville (where the coal was transhipped to the canal-boats) about forty years ago, the first extensive opening of the mine being in 1831. The first President of the company was Mr. Samuel D. Ingham, Secretary of the Treasury under General Jackson. The trains in those *primitive* days consisted of fifteen cars of small tonnage, and were drawn southward by small engines, carrying on the down trip several mules to aid in the return. The business of the road gradually increased from year to year, until from being the means of transporting a small quantity of coal for the company's own mines at this point, in 1837, amounting to 33,617 tons, it became the outlet for numerous operations in the neighborhood, carrying nearly 750,000 tons of coal in 1859.

Since the removal to Weatherly of the machine- and

car- repair-shops, formerly located here, the business of the place is almost exclusively that connected with the mining of coal in the neighborhood. At these shops there were built, under the superintendence of Hopkin Thomas and Aaron H. Van Cleve, some of the first four-wheeled and six-wheeled locomotives ever constructed in the State. It may be interesting to note in this connection that Mr. Thomas was the first to introduce the burning of anthracite coal in locomotives. There are churches belonging to the Presbyterians and Methodists. The population is 600.

LEVISTON.

This town derives its name from Hosea J. Levis, one of the original directors of the Beaver Meadow Company.

It has two breakers, owned by W. T. Carter & Co., with a capacity of 180,000 tons per annum, employing 325 men and boys; also one belonging to Ely, Martin & Co., which has a capacity of 40,000 tons per annum, and gives employment to 70 men and boys.

JEANESVILLE.

Coal was first discovered in the Jeanesville tract by James D. Gallup, an old pioneer explorer in these parts. The property was once held in whole or in part by Joseph H. Newbold, and was bought for about $20,000 by Joseph Jeanes, of Philadelphia, and several others, who, in order to utilize their purchase, let it to William Milnes, at a rental of twenty-five cents for every ton of coal shipped. Mr. Milnes went to work energetically, and soon had the colliery in operation; and in 1855 the owners were receiving of him for rent about $40,000 per annum. His lease lasted for twenty years; and, as nearly as can be estimated, not less than one and a half million of tons were shipped by Milnes from it, since which the property has passed into the hands of the Spring Mountain Coal Company, by whom probably not less than one million tons of coal have been shipped from the same property, and there seems to be no cessation or diminution of the supply. A town of 1500 inhabitants has grown up on the property, all of whom able to work, both men and boys, are employed by the company, to the number of from 450 to 500. There are three breakers, whose united capacity is 250,000 tons per annum.

The village is supplied with water by water-works erected at the expense of the company. A machine-shop and foundry is carried on in connection with the works, employing about 40 men, and turning out an amount of finished work of probably $100,000 per annum,—that is, in work and material. This shop consumes say 1000 tons of coal per annum, and about 400 tons of pig-iron, besides other material, and is in the occupancy of S. Cornelison & Co.

There are Methodist and Congregational churches here, besides a spacious public hall. One mile to the west, the Beaver Brook Company have two slopes and two breakers, with a capacity of about 2500 tons per week.

AUDENRIED.

The works of the Honey Brook Coal Company are located here. They consist of three slopes and three breakers (which latter are said to be the largest and best-constructed in the Beaver Meadow Region) having a capacity of 3000 tons per day, and giving employment to about 750 men and boys.

There are churches belonging to the Welsh Congregationalists and Baptists, the Presbyterians, and the Methodists, as also a large public hall. Population, 1500. About three-quarters of a mile to the east, at Tresckow, the South Spring Mountain Company have two slopes and one breaker, with a capacity of 500 tons per day, and employing 500 men and boys.

At Yorktown, immediately adjoining Audenried, the Spring Brook Coal Company have two slopes and two breakers, with a capacity of 800 tons per day, and employing 420 men and boys.

HAZLETON DIVISION.

For Penn Haven, Black Creek Junction, Weatherly, and Hazle Creek Bridge, see Beaver Meadow Division.

MILLER'S.

Near by are several saw-mills in operation, and some abandoned powder-mills.

LUMBER-YARD.

The point at which this division diverges to Jeddo and Eckley.

TUNNEL.

So named from the tunnel (1017 feet long) constructed at this point through Council Ridge, which divides the Hazleton and Black Creek Coal Basins. Formerly the ridge was crossed by a zigzag track over its summit.

ECKLEY.

The site of this village (formerly called Fillmore) was, in 1854, a perfect wilderness. At that time Sharpe, Leisenring & Co. commenced explorations on the tract to ascertain the thickness and extent of the coal-veins. They were soon well satisfied of their value, and, as the first step towards making a settlement, built a saw-mill, for the conversion of the forests into dwellings. Since then the town has steadily grown and improved, until now it has a population of about 1200. The Episcopalians, Presbyterians, and Roman Catholics each have a neat church building.

The general arrangement of the place is noteworthy. No mining town in the State has anything more complete. The houses are located in four graded sections, the cottages of the proprietors being in one, those of the boss laborers and contractors in another, those of the miners in a third, those of the laborers and slate-pickers in a fourth. The houses are neat-looking and comfortable, and have ample garden-room in their rear. A short distance out of town, water-works have been erected to supply the village and feed the boilers. A saw-mill also is still in operation. The collieries here, belonging to Sharpe, Weiss & Co., and operated by them upon a lease now about expiring, are known by the name of Council Ridge, so called from a mountain near by, whereon was held the Indian council of war which immediately preceded the massacre in the Wyoming Valley, an account of which will be found on pp. 91–3. The locating of the openings was done principally under the direction of Mr. Asa L. Foster, one of the most honored pioneers of this region (now deceased), whose judgment in such matters was always greatly valued. The works consist of three slopes and two breakers, the combined capacity of which is about 150,000 tons per annum. The number of hands employed is about 200 men and boys. The population of the town is 900.

Eckley is situated at one of the highest points in Northern Pennsylvania, on the dividing line for the waters flowing on the east to the Lehigh and on the west to the Susquehanna. Some of the views in the neighborhood are especially extensive and picturesque. To the northwest of the town, on the summit of Buck Mountain, the Conyngham and Butler Valleys lie stretched out before the eye in landscapes of rich variety. Of a clear day the Susquehanna Valley is easily seen through the opening made by the Nescopec

Notch. To the northeast a beautiful view is had of the upper portion of the Lehigh Valley and the Pocono Mountain, with the end of Buck and Green Mountains in the vicinity of White Haven.

FOUNDRY.

There is located here a foundry, whose principal work is connected with repairs to the mines in the vicinity.

JEDDO.

This town derives its name from the interest taken at the time in Commodore Perry's expedition to Japan. In 1850 Coffin & Yost erected a saw-mill and manufactured a large quantity of white pine lumber.

In the winter of 1858 a charter was obtained for the Union Improvement Company, covering the whole of the original tract now owned chiefly by A. S. and E. Roberts. Wm. Lilly and G. B. Markle leased the land in 1859 (A. Pardee & Co. being interested with them), and immediately commenced the mining of coal, shipping during the first year 50,000 tons. Since then, their operations have been largely increased, there being now three slopes and three breakers, with a combined capacity of 1000 tons per day, employing about 350 men and boys. The veins worked here are the Mammoth and the Buck Mountain. A steam saw-mill is also located here. Population, 750.

Jeddo is the passenger station for several important

towns in the neighborhood, to which the railroad is extended by branches for the transportation of coal. Among these may be mentioned—

Drifton, where there are three drifts, in which the coal is still worked above the water-level. Here there is a large and very complete breaker, with a capacity of 150,000 tons per annum. This, with several other collieries in the neighborhood, is owned by Judge Chas. S. Coxe, of Philadelphia.

Woodside, where there is one breaker, with a capacity of 50,000 tons per annum, employing 50 men and boys.

Highland, where there is, in addition to a steam saw-mill, one slope, with a capacity of 75,000 tons per annum, employing about 100 men and boys.

On the Lehigh Luzerne Branch there are, besides Ebervale,—

Harleigh, where there are two breakers, with a capacity of 150,000 tons per annum, employing 150 men and boys;

Lattimer, where there are two breakers, with a capacity of 200,000 tons per annum, employing 250 men and boys; and

Milnesville, where there is one breaker, with a capacity of 75,000 tons, employing 100 men and boys.

EBERVALE.

In addition to a saw-mill located here, there is a colliery with three slopes and two breakers, having a capacity of 250,000 tons per annum, and employing 250 men and boys.

STOCKTON.

This town is named in honor of Commodore Robert F. Stockton, whose liberal aid in the development of this region has already been mentioned. The East Sugarloaf Coal Mines situated here (owned now by Linderman, Skeer & Co.) were opened in 1850, and are worked by four slopes. Their united capacity is about 350,000 tons per annum, and they employ 500 hands. The improvements in the village are upon an unusually extensive scale, evidenced in the permanency and adaptability of the machinery and fixtures connected with the establishment.

In December, 1870, through a falling in of an abandoned working, two blocks of houses, with their inmates, were wholly engulfed. Seven lives were lost by this catastrophe. Five of the bodies still remain buried there, all efforts to recover them proving ineffectual.

Population, 1100. The only church in the town is that which belongs to the Methodists.

HAZLETON.

This is one of the handsomest and most enterprising towns in the coal region. It is situated on what is known as the dividing ridge of the Lehigh and Susquehanna Rivers, the waters in the western part of the town running into the Susquehanna, while those in the eastern part flow into the Lehigh. Its name is derived from Hazle Creek, at the head of which it is located, and which is doubtless so called from a kind of hazel-bush which grows abundantly along its banks. It is situated eighteen hundred feet above tide-water, and about twelve hundred feet above the Susquehanna at Berwick, and is one of the highest inhabited portions of Northern Pennsylvania. It was settled in 1836, and incorporated in 1857. Its growth has been steady and rapid, the number of inhabitants being at present about 5000, in addition to which there is a large population in the numerous other towns lying in close proximity. The principal street is one hundred feet in width and a mile in length, lined on either side with good and substantial buildings. The handsome residence and grounds of Ario Pardee (to whom this whole region is so largely indebted for its present state of wonderful prosperity) occupy a prominent position.

Hazleton has become quite a place of summer resort, the healthfulness of the locality and the delightful coolness of the atmosphere attracting many of the inhabitants of our seaboard cities. The town is well supplied, from works owned by the railroad company, with pure spring-water from an adjoining hill. A gas company has recently been organized, and has commenced operations.

There are church buildings owned by the Roman Catholics, the Presbyterians, the Episcopalians, the Methodists, the Albright Methodists, the Lutherans, the Dutch Reformed, and the German Reformed. There are published here one daily and two weekly newspapers. The town-hall is a large and imposing building, with fine store-rooms underneath and lodge-rooms above. Besides the extensive shops belonging to the railroad company, there are planing-mills, chair-factory, foundry and machine-shop, carriage-factory, etc. There are two savings-banks, having discounting privileges, with a combined capital of $250,000.

The following are the dimensions of the railroad company's shops:

Machine-shop . . .	450 by 50	feet.	
Foundry	104 by 56	"	
Car-wheel-shop . . .	80 by 36	"	with a wing 36 ft. square.
Boiler-shop . . .	102 by 52	"	
Forge or steam-hammer-shop	50 by 50	"	
Blacksmith-shop . .	80 by 40	"	with a wing 75 by 35 feet.
Car-shop	95 by 50	"	with a wing 95 by 63 feet.

The round-house is a semicircle, having twenty-one stables and a fifty-two feet turn-table. Besides the general work of manufacture and repair for the Company, these shops are largely engaged in making stationary engines, pumps, breakers, etc. for the surrounding collieries. All the locomotives running on this division of the road were also made here, and bear ample testimony to the excellent workmanship employed in their construction.

At these works there were used during the year 1872, of—

Pig-iron	2001	tons.
Bar-iron	344,722	pounds.
Boiler-iron	191,009	"
Russia sheet-iron	5276	"
Pig-lead	6952	"
Pig-tin	3123	"
Ingot-copper	17,675	"
Nails and spikes	16,900	"
Rivets	21,170	"
Screen-iron	163,896	"
Tank-iron	25,707	"
Steel-plate	21,295	"

Sheet-brass	910 pounds.
Coal	2,690 tons.
Lard-oil	1,410 gallons.
Machine-oil	3,330 "

The total value of material used was $235,441.68, and the amount of wages paid was $172,916. In addition to that done for the Company, work was also done here for other parties to the amount of $122,000. The number of men employed was 272. During the year seven locomotives were built and twenty-six repaired.

In and immediately around Hazleton there are seven collieries, operated by A. Pardee & Co., numbering eight slopes and seven breakers, the united capacity of which is 16,000 tons per week. In them there are employed 1200 men and boys. Near the Company's shops is said to be the deepest mine in the United States. It is 970 feet perpendicular, and 600 yards on the slope.

Three miles and a half to the west of the borough is the Mount Pleasant Colliery, consisting of one slope and one breaker, the capacity of which is 1600 tons per week, employing 100 men and boys.

A mile farther is the Humboldt Colliery, consisting of one slope and one breaker, with a capacity of 2000 tons per week, and employing 120 men and boys.

The first shipment of coal from this neighborhood was in 1838, by the Hazleton and Laurel Hill Companies. Now the weekly shipment by the Hazleton Division proper amounts to 60,000 tons per week. The veins mostly worked are the Big (white ash) and the Buck Mountain (red ash), with other smaller veins intervening. The Big Vein is about thirty-three feet between the rocks, and the Buck Mountain about fifteen feet.

By the recent construction of the Danville, Hazleton, and Wilkes-Barre Railroad, direct communication is had with Danville, Sunbury, and intermediate points.

CRANBERRY.

The location of one of the collieries operated by A. Pardee & Co., included in the statement of their capacity, etc., under the head of HAZLETON.

CONYNGHAM.

Situated at the top of the mountain overlooking the Conyngham Valley, which is one of the most beautiful valleys in the State.

TOMHICKEN.

The junction of the Hazleton Division with the Danville, Hazleton, and Wilkes-Barre Railroad.

MAHANOY DIVISION.

HARTZ'S.

A former stopping-place (named after Col. Jacob Hartz, an old and prominent settler of this region) on the turnpike from Wilkes-Barre to Mauch Chunk. It contains a foundry for mine-pipes, a grist-mill, and saw-mill. Considerable prop-timber is obtained here.

GERHARD'S.

There are located here a saw-mill and grist-mills. It is also a shipping-place for lumber.

STEWART'S.

A stopping-place on the wagon-road from Tamaqua to Beaver Meadow. Depot for timber and farmers' supplies.

SWITCH BACK.

So called from a plane which formerly existed here a short distance up the gorge, connecting with the Catawissa Railroad, extending by a switch-back from the foot of the plane to what is now Quakake Junction. At this point the railroad crosses the Little Schuylkill with an embankment, handsomely arched, eighty-five feet high, the masonry of which is especially fine. Several powder-mills are situated in the immediate neighborhood.

QUAKAKE JUNCTION.

At this point the Mahanoy Division of the Lehigh Valley Railroad connects with the Catawissa and Williamsport Division of the Philadelphia and Reading Railroad, and passengers going north change cars for Catawissa, Rupert, Bloomsburg, Danville, Muncy, Williamsport, etc. The ascent over the mountain (a spur of the Broad Mountain) is on a grade of seventy-six feet, and affords to the lover of beautiful scenery a landscape rarely equaled in Pennsylvania. It is only less extensive than that furnished near Wilkes-Barre, of the Wyoming Valley, with which, in its several charming outlines, it is often compared. The rapid transit of the cars gives us too short a glimpse of a panorama which will well repay a more careful study, whereby its many points of interest can be more leisurely enjoyed.

DELANO.

Here are located extensive and substantial shops belonging to the Lehigh Valley Railroad Company, and residences of firemen, brakesmen, and others employed in their service. The town was settled in 1864, and was named after Warren Delano, the President of the New Boston Coal Company, whose mines are in the neighborhood.

The dimensions of the several shops are as follows:

Machine-shop	100 by 140 feet.
Smith-shop	54 by 80 "
Boiler-shop	35 by 70 "
Carpenter-shop	25 by 130 "
Tin-shop	24 by 30 "
Tool-shop	20 by 20 "

The number of men employed in these various departments is 130. During the year 1872, there were used of material as follows:

Cast-iron	280,000 pounds.
Wrought-iron	80,000 "
Sheet-iron	75,000 "
Spring steel	20,000 "
Copper	3,000 "
Babbitt-metal	1,000 "

The chief item of work done here is the building, rebuilding, and repairing of locomotives. During the past year two engines were rebuilt, and sixty-seven old ones repaired. They are fully equal to any employed on the road. Total cost of material used, $30,000; total cost of labor, $65,000. Total mileage, 1,568,864. Number of gallons of oil used, 10,000; of pounds of waste, 25,000.

The engine-house is 64 by 250 feet, and has accommodations for sixteen engines.

About a mile to the west of the town is situated the Pine Creek Colliery, employing 40 men and boys, and having a capacity of 150 tons per day.

MAHANOY CITY.

The records of the spot upon which the town is situated can be traced as far back as January 31st, 1789, at which time Christian Barrenstein made an application for fifty acres of land, upon which a warrant was issued from John Lukens, Surveyor-General, the territory being at that time comprised within Berks County. Then followed the Kunkle survey in 1792, that of the Delano Land Company in 1793, and that of the Kear and Patterson estate in 1794. Others followed immediately after, so that but little land was left in the hands of the Commonwealth in this vicinity at the beginning of the present century.

The first settlement was made between the years 1800 and 1810, and consisted in part of a saw-mill and dam, of which traces were visible east of Fifth Street in the early days of the town. In 1810, Peter Knalb erected a tavern near the site of the present hay-scales, which appears to be the first house of which anything positive is remembered. Between 1810 and 1820 several dwellings were erected on the McNeal tract, and afterwards on the North Mahanoy. For a number of years the principal business was that of lumbering and shingle-making, which was carried on to a considerable extent. In 1858 the town was first laid out (its Indian name being derived from the creek running through it), there being at that time but one house within its proposed limits. It was incorporated in 1864. Its growth until 1861 was steady but slow; but from 1862 to 1866 the progress was remarkably rapid, buildings arising as if by magic. Since then the town has continued to grow and improve, and the spirit of enterprise bids fair to outlast many older settlements. Its present population is about 6000, in addition to which there are several thousands of inhabitants living in the numerous smaller towns in the neighborhood. The discovery and development of the coal-fields immediately surrounding the town have, of course, been the chief means of accelerating its prosperity. At the present time there are within its limits, and near by, twenty collieries, each having on an average a capacity of 250 tons per day, and employing 200 men and boys. The capital invested in them will amount to at least $1,500,000.

Among the manufacturing establishments in the borough are an iron-foundry, a pottery, a screen factory, a boiler-factory, and a steam-flouring mill. There is a national bank, with a capital of $100,000, and a savings-bank, with an authorized capital of $150,000. Two weekly newspapers are published here. The town is well supplied with water, and steps have lately been taken to improve the streets and light them. The main street is a fine avenue, eighty feet wide and a mile in length. There are church buildings belonging to the following denominations: Presbyterian, Reformed, Methodist Episcopal, Primitive Methodist, Evangelical Methodist, Protestant Episcopal, Welsh Congregational, Roman Catholic (Irish and German), Baptist (Welsh and English), and Lutheran (German and English).

MYERSVILLE.

Junction of the branch road from Mahanoy City. The Hoffman Colliery is situated here, having one breaker, with a capacity of 200 tons per day.

YATESVILLE.

Contains the McNeal Coal Company's Collieries, comprising two breakers with a combined capacity of 1200 tons per day, employing 450 men and boys, with a capital of $500,000. The Knickerbocker Anthracite Coal Company also has a breaker here, with a capacity of 500 tons per day, giving employment to 220 men and boys. Population, including Barry's, 1000.

SHENANDOAH.

This flourishing borough is a fair example of the rapidity with which many of the towns in this region have grown. In 1863, the spot which it at present occupies was a comparative wilderness, the only sign of civilization being a solitary old house, with an acre or two of cleared ground. It was incorporated in 1866, and its population now is nearly 5000. It derives its name from the Shenandoah Creek, which passes through it. The trade of the Catawissa Valley, a fine agricultural district, mainly centres here, and is of growing importance. The main support of the place, however, is the coal trade, and in that interest its prospects are thought to be second to no other town in Schuylkill County, some of the finest veins ever worked being found here. The Shenandoah coal-basin is about four miles in length by one mile in width, and the number of active operations within its limits is about twelve, several of which are of very recent date. The following is a summary of the number of tons shipped during the year 1872, showing a large increase over that of former years.

Colorado Colliery	127,250
Plank Ridge Colliery	133,103
Shenandoah Colliery	44,511
Keely Run Colliery	106,919
Shenandoah City Colliery	73,718
William Penn Colliery	89,300
Indian Ridge Colliery	81,915
Turkey Run Colliery	77,469
West Shenandoah Colliery	8,726
Kohinoor Colliery	104,743
Girardville (2d col.)	103,760
Lehigh Colliery	55,500
Total	1,006,914

Besides the usual number of stores and hotels, there are two banks, with a combined capital of $150,000, a weekly newspaper, a foundry, and a machine-shop. Of churches, there are the Roman Catholic (Irish and German), Methodist, Presbyterian, German Lutheran, Welsh Congregational, Welsh Presbyterian, and Welsh Baptist. The Episcopalians and the Primitive and German (Albright) Methodists also hold service on stated occasions, but are as yet without buildings of their own. A handsome and commodious public school-house is under contract, and will cost, it is thought, from $15,000 to $20,000. Permission has been obtained from the Legislature to borrow $25,000 for improvement of the streets, etc., and the authorities expect shortly to put the work through.

RAVEN RUN.

Here are situated the Girard Mammoth Colliery, with a capacity of 600 tons per day, and employing 210 men and boys, and the Cuyler Colliery, employing 160 men and boys, with a capacity of 400 tons per day. Both were started in October, 1866.

From this point a branch road runs to Montana (a thriving town on the turnpike to Pottsville), where the Reno Colliery is located, which has a capacity of 700 tons per day.

Raven Run is also the outlet chosen for the New York and Middle Coal Field Railroad Company, whose road, partially built in the most costly and approved manner about twenty years ago, was subsequently abandoned. A fine view may be obtained here of Mount Carmel and the vicinity. Population, about 600.

CENTRALIA.

This town was settled about 1853, and incorporated in 1866, and contains a population of over 2000. The Presbyterians, the Roman Catholics, the Methodists, and the Episcopalians, each have a church building of their own, and a Welsh service is also held. The collieries of Messrs. Robert Gorrelle & Co., Norton, Audenried & Co., and Ryan & Co., situated here, have a combined capacity of about 400,000 tons per annum.

MOUNT CARMEL.

This is the terminus of the Mahanoy Branch of the Lehigh Valley Railroad, which connects at this point with the Shamokin Branch of the Northern Central Railway.

It was settled in 1853, incorporated in 1862, and contains about 2000 inhabitants. There are in the neighborhood six collieries, whose united capacity is about 600,000 tons per annum. There are also located here a machine-shop, foundry, and shovel-factory.

There are church buildings owned by the Lutherans, Methodists, and Roman Catholics. Services are also held by the Episcopalians, Baptists, and United Brethren of Christ.

APPENDIX A.

COAL.

A FEW statistics of the anthracite coal trade are subjoined, as giving the reader a general idea of the enormous proportions to which it has grown. They are copied from the *Miners' Journal Register* for 1873.

The following gives the number of collieries, etc. in the different regions:

	No. of Collieries.	No. of Shafts.	No. of Slopes.	No. of Drifts, etc.
Schuylkill County . . .	164	13	141	102
Northumberland County	33		18	52
Columbia County . . .	8		7	4
Dauphin County . . .	4		4	
Luzerne East	80	46	21	68
Luzerne West	102	31	43	42
Lehigh Region	46	1	59	12
	437	91	293	280

The following is the quantity mined in 1872:

	Sent to Market. Official.	Home Consumption. Estimated.	Total Production.
Schuylkill and Columbia Counties	4,455,813	900,000	5,355,813
Northumberland County	1,221,327	170,000	1,391,327
Lehigh Region . .	3,610,374	500,000	4,110,374
Wyoming Region . .	9,191,171	1,500,000	10,691,171
Lyken's Valley . . .	450,328	40,000	490,328
	18,929,013	3,110,000	22,039,013

The quantity of coal mined in Great Britain during 1872 was 120,000,000 tons, of which there were exported 13,211,961 tons.

The casualties in 1872 were as follows:

	Killed.	Injured.
Schuylkill County	65	216
Northumberland County . . .	10	26
Columbia County	7	10
Dauphin County	8	13
Lehigh Region	25	38
Wyoming Region	107	308
	222	611

APPENDIX B.

IRON.

It is not positively known when or where iron was first made in the United States, but the attention of the first settlers of the British Colonies was very early directed (no doubt by the previous knowledge of the Indians) to the iron ore with which the country abounds, and in various sections furnaces were soon erected for its conversion into metal. Perhaps the first production from native ore in Pennsylvania was at the Coventry Forge, in Chester County, in 1720.

It was not until after the discovery of the use of anthracite coal in furnaces, that the foundations of the immense establishments were laid which have given to this trade its present importance. Prior to this time the ore was converted into metal by the use of bituminous coal, charcoal, and coke. This process was far less economical than was desirable, and therefore when the value of anthracite for ordinary purposes of fuel was fairly tested, its adaptation to smelting uses was tried, and, after a series of reverses and a period of general incredulity, gladly hailed as a great saving in both metal and fuel. This success added largely not only to the prosperity of the iron trade, but of the coal trade also.

Up to about 1833 the cold blast was exclusively employed in the furnaces. At that time the Rev. Frederic W. Geisenhainer, of Schuylkill County, after various experiments in the treatment of anthracite with the hot blast, obtained a patent for the same, and in 1835 he made iron by this process in a small stack near Pottsville.

The Lehigh Valley has now become the largest producing region in the country, having at the present time more than forty furnaces in operation, with an annual capacity of over 400,000 tons. Quite a contrast to this is afforded in the list of articles transported by the Lehigh Canal in 1836, when there were carried of iron only 1197 tons, while of *whisky* there were 641 tons! The quantity of pig-metal manufactured in the United States during 1872 is estimated as follows:

Anthracite	1,137,010	tons.
Raw coal and coke	742,500	"
Charcoal	498,500	"
	2,378,010	

In 1810 it is computed that there were 30,000 tons produced.

The product of the English furnaces during the year 1872 is estimated to have been 7,000,000 tons.

Touching the question of who first used anthracite coal in the manufacture of iron, the following documents are submitted. Reference has already been made to this subject under the head of Mauch Chunk, where it is stated upon good authority that an attempt in this direction prior to the dates below mentioned was made at Mauch Chunk by members of the Lehigh Coal and Navigation Company.

The first letter, originally published in the *American Manufacturer*, is as follows:

"CATASAUQUA, PA., Feb. 23d, 1872.

"B. F. H. LYNN, Esq.:

"DEAR SIR,—The question of who was the first person to use anthracite coal for smelting iron, is difficult to answer; but I will give you a few facts, from which you can draw your own conclusions.

"In the year 1825, while manager of the Yniscedwin Works, South Wales (where I was from 1817 to 1839), I built a blast furnace of 9 feet bosh and 30 feet high to make experiments with anthracite coal, which abounded in that neighboroood, while we brought coke 14 miles by canal to smelt ore with. This furnace was blown in with coke in 1826, and the anthracite introduced first one-sixteenth part of the fuel and gradually advanced to one-half, when we had to stop and blow out. It was a failure.

"In 1832, the same furnace was altered to 45 feet high and 11 feet bosh, and the same experiment tried, with the same result.

"In 1836, hot-blast ovens were built to this furnace, according to Mr. Neilson's patent for hot blast, of Glasgow, Scotland, and on the 5th of February, 1837, anthracite iron was made, and quite successfully, and in that I claim to have been the first person to obtain successful results,—at least as far as I know or ever heard of.

"By an agreement in writing, made with the Lehigh Coal & Navigation Company (which agreement I still have in my possession), I came to this country in the spring of 1839, at which time I found a small furnace at South Easton, worked by a Mr. Van Buren, who was endeavoring to make iron with anthracite coal. It was run some ten days or two weeks, when it chilled, and proved a failure, both financially and as a furnace. There was another at Mauch Chunk, owned by three or four men,—a Mr. Bauhm, a Mr. Gitto, and a Mr. Lathrop (the latter I think still being at Trenton, N. J.). This furnace was chilled up in about one week after blowing-in.

"At the same time there was another building at Pottsville, by Mr. Lyman. I received a communication from this gentleman by the hand of the President of the Lehigh Crane Iron Company, for whom I was building the first furnace at this place. This letter urged me to come to Pottsville. I visited him in August, 1839, and furnished him with plans of in-wall, bosh, hearth, etc., and continued to visit him about once a month until the furnace was completed, which was in January, 1840. Then I was so engaged here that I could not remain with him long enough to put it in blast. He accordingly obtained the services of Mr. B.

Perry, who blew it in, as founder. They made iron for some weeks,—I am not able to say how many,—but, the machinery not being strong, they broke down, and I believe the furnace chilled up, though I will not be positive on this point, as it might have been blown out.

"On the 4th of July, 1840, I made the first iron on this plan in our first furnace here, and kept it running month after month and year after year. In 1841, I built the second, in 1846, the third, in 1849, the fourth and fifth, and in 1860, the sixth, and there are now in this Valley 46 anthracite furnaces, producing over 400,000 tons of pig-iron annually.

"I am sorry I have to write this so long, but could not well make it intelligible if shorter. When next I see you I will take pleasure in telling you of scores of experiments made with anthracite coal. I have been in the blast-furnace business sixty years the 12th of April next, and forty-five to fifty of these years I have been experimenting with anthracite. I care very little about the glory,—who was, or who is the successful candidate,—as men's praises are like shadows.

"You may use this, as I fear no contradiction. I have written nothing but plain facts, but not one-tenth of what might be said did necessity call for it.

"I should be glad to hear from you.

"Yours very truly,

"David Thomas.

"P.S.—Mr. Richards did not buy the Mauch Chunk Furnace until 1842 or 1843, and he used charcoal in it."

We give below a letter from Mr. James Pott, of Harrisburg, to the editor of the *Coal and Iron Record:*

"In No. 1 of vol. i. of your journal, you give a sketch of David Thomas, in the course of which you say, 'He was the first man to demonstrate the practicability of using anthracite in smelting iron ores. . . . . And of all this magnificent industry, the furnace started by Mr. Thomas, at Pottsville, *less* than thirty years ago, has been the pioneer.'

"My object in addressing you is, not to detract from the credit due Mr. Thomas for the perfection to which he has carried this business, but to correct what I believe to be an error. My father, John Pott, used anthracite coal to smelt iron ore in his furnace (Manheim Iron Works), on the West Branch of the Schuylkill, as early as 1836–7: first in connection with charcoal, then with wood cut short, like stove-wood, and finally, by making some change in the interior of the furnace, with anthracite alone,—a hot blast having already been attached.

"These experiments, running through several years, demonstrated to his entire satisfaction the practicability of using anthracite in reducing iron ore; but about 1838–39 the works stood idle for a year or more, when, in the year 1840, he made preparation to enlarge the furnace and to construct it on different principles, which its former size would not admit of. In the early spring of 1841, and before the work was completed, came a terrible ice-freshet, which swept away everything, tearing up the very foundations of forge and furnace; and this was the end of the 'Manheim Iron Works.' A few years later my father sold the property, and in 1844 removed to Bedford (now Fulton) County, Pa., where, for several years, he conducted the 'Hanover Iron Works.' The paralyzation of this industry, following the adoption of the tariff of 1846, compelled him to abandon the business in 1847, and thenceforth he devoted himself to agriculture and milling until he died, in November, 1856.

"From early life, my father had been engaged in the manufacture of iron, and so also was his father (John Pott), who, in 1807, built 'Greenwood Furnace' on the 'Island,' where Atkins' extensive furnaces, at Pottsville, now are.

"Mr. Thomas is a public benefactor, and deserves great credit for his energy and enterprise in carrying forward this business to such perfection and success; but I feel that it is but just to correct what I believe to be an error, and to claim for John Pott the credit of having first successfully demonstrated the 'practicability of using anthracite in smelting iron ores,' and for little 'Manheim Furnace' the distinction of having been the 'pioneer' in what has since grown into such wondrous proportions under the skill and tact of Mr. Thomas.

"I remember well hearing my father often remark that he was the first to use and demonstrate the adaptability of anthracite to blast-furnaces, and that others—the name of Mr. Thomas being mentioned in his observations—had carried it forward to perfect success.

"At the time of the destruction of the works, the supply of anthracite for the reconstructed furnace had been contracted for, and a large quantity had already been delivered on the furnace 'bank,'—a pile so large as to seem to my youthful eyes like a mountain of coal.

"You will not blame me, sir, for being a little sensitive on this subject. I have not at hand my father's books, from which to obtain data, and am writing from memory, making the 'Hard-Cider' campaign in 1840 and the great freshet in 1841 the points from which I calculate. If I am in error, I am willing to be corrected."

The following was published in the *Mauch Chunk Democrat:*

"TRENTON, N. J., March 26th, 1872.

"MR. EDITOR,—Some unknown person (a friend, I suppose) has sent me an article of about half a column in length, clipped from some newspaper, upon the margin of which I find written in pencil the question: 'How about this?'

"The article begins thus: 'For some time past there has been a discussion going on in regard to the credit of making the first anthracite iron in the United States, — Mr. David Thomas, of the Thomas Iron Works, Mr. John Richards, deceased, once of the old Mauch Chunk Furnace, and Mr. Lyman, of Pottsville, each having their friends to advocate their separate claims to the honor.'

"Next follows a letter from Mr. David Thomas, relating his experience and knowledge of the matter in question, in the course of which he makes the following statement: 'There was another [furnace] at Mauch Chunk, owned by three or four men,—a Mr. Bauhm, a Mr. Gitto. and a Mr. Lathrop (the latter, I think, is still living at Trenton, N. J.). This furnace was chilled up in about one week after blowing-in.'

"Mr. Thomas's memory must certainly have failed him, or he was misinformed in regard to the Mauch

Chunk Furnace, as will appear evident from the following extracts from—

"'Notes on the Use of Anthracite in the Manufacture of Iron; with some Remarks on its Evaporative Power. By Walter R. Johnson, A.M., Boston, 1841.'

"'The furnace at Mauch Chunk, which stands at the head of the preceding table, is believed to have been the first in this country at which any considerable success was attained in the smelting of iron with anthracite.* Their ore produced was of various, but mostly inferior, qualities, owing probably to deficiency of blast. The blowing cylinders were of wood (single acting), and at the speed employed did not furnish over 700 cubic feet of air per minute.

"'Their apparatus for hot blast was at first defective, and was afterwards placed at the tunnel-head, where it could be seen as well regulated as though managed in separate ovens, with an independent fire. Hence, even of the limited supply of air taken into the bellows, a considerable portion must have been lost by leakage, and by escapes at the open tuyeres there applied.'

"'BEAVER MEADOW, PA., November 9th, 1840.

"'SIR,—Agreeably to a request of Col. Henry High, of Reading, I send you the following hastily-written statement of the experiments made by Baughman, Guiteau & Co., in the smelting of iron ore with anthracite coal as a fuel.

"'During the fall and winter of the year 1837, Messrs. Joseph Baughman, Julius Guiteau, and Henry High, of

* Beaver Meadow (Pa.) coal.

Reading, made their first experiment in smelting iron ore with anthracite coal, in an old furnace at Mauch Chunk, temporarily fitted up for the purpose.

"'They used about 80 per cent. of anthracite, and the result was such as to surprise those who witnessed it (for it was considered an impossibility even by iron-masters), and to encourage the persons engaged in it to go on. In order, therefore, to test the matter more thoroughly, they built a furnace on a small scale near Mauch Chunk Weigh Lock, which was completed during the month of July, 1838. Dimensions: Stack 21½ feet high, 22 feet square at base, boshes 5½ feet across, hearth 14 to 16 inches square, and 4 feet 9 inches from the dam-stone to the back. The blowing apparatus consisted of two cylinders, each 6 feet diameter; a receiver, same diameter, and about 2½ feet deep; stroke 11 inches. Each piston making from 12 to 15 strokes per minute. An overshot water-wheel, diameter 14 feet, length of buckets 3½ feet; number of buckets, 36; revolutions per minute, from 12 to 15.

"'The blast was applied August 27th, and the furnace kept in blast until September 10th, when they were obliged to stop in consequence of the apparatus for heating the blast proving to be too temporary. Several tons of iron were produced of Nos. 2 and 3 quality. I do not recollect the proportion of anthracite coal used. Temperature of the blast did not exceed 200° Fahrenheit.

"'A new and good apparatus for heating the blast was next procured (it was at this time I became a partner in the firm of B. G. & Co.), consisting of 200 feet in length of cast-iron pipes 1½ inches; it was placed in a brick chamber, at the tunnel-head, and heated by a flame issuing thence. The blast was again applied about the last of November, 1838, and the furnace worked remarkably well for five weeks, exclusively with anthracite coal; we were obliged, however, for want of ore, to blow out on the 12th of January, 1839. During this experiment, our doors were open to the public, and we were watched very closely both day and night, for men could hardly believe what they saw with their own eyes, so incredulous was the public in regard to the matter at this time; some iron-masters expressed themselves astonished that a furnace would work, whilst using *unburnt, unwashed, frozen* ore, such as was put into our furnace.

"'The amount of iron produced was about 1½ tons per day, when working best, of Nos. 1, 2, and 3 quality. The average temperature of the blast was 400° Fahrenheit.

"'The following season we enlarged the hearth to 19 by 20 inches, and 5 feet 3 inches from the dam-stone to the back of the hearth, and on July 26th the furnace was again put in blast, and continued in blast until November 2d, 1839, a few days after the dissolution of our firm, when it was blown out in good order.

"'For about three months we used no other fuel than anthracite, and produced about 100 tons of iron of good Nos. 1, 2, and 3 quality. When working best, the furnace produced two tons a day.

"'Temperature of the blast 400° to 600° Fahrenheit. The following ores were used by us, viz.: "Pipe ore," from Miller's mines, a few miles from Allentown; "brown hæmatite," commonly called "*top mine*," or surface ore; "rock ore" from Dickerson mine in New Jersey; and "Williams Township ore" in Northampton County. The last-mentioned ore produced a very strong iron and most beautiful cinder.

"'The above experiments were prosecuted under the most discouraging circumstances, and if we gain anything by it, it can only be the credit of acting the part of pioneers in a praiseworthy undertaking.

"'Most respectfully, sir,
"'Your obedient servant,
"'F. C. LOWTHROP.

"'Prof. WALTER R. JOHNSON, Philadelphia.'"

"'Correct copy from the book:
"'JOHN WISE,
"'Librarian Franklin Institute,
"'Philadelphia, Pa.'

"As an evidence of the reliability of the work from which the above extracts were taken, I would remind your readers that its author, in 1844, published, by order of Congress, a 'Report on the Different Varieties of Coal' in order to determine their evaporative powers.

"Respectfully yours,
"F. C. LOWTHROP."

Subsequently the following appeared in the *Bethlehem Times*:

"The following documents have been placed in our hands for publication, and we hope that any persons who may have facts or evidence of facts which will throw light on the subject will forward them to us, that we may lay them before our readers. Some time since, we published the following paragraph:

"'The first successful use of anthracite coal for the smelting of iron was in 1839, at the Pioneer Furnace, at Pottsville, Pa. It had been tried on the Lehigh in 1826, but was unsuccessful.'

"To some extent to corroborate this statement, which was called in question in private conversation by some gentlemen, a friend handed us the following letter and petition to the Legislature, with the request to publish them, as throwing light on the subject. We are unable to give the presentation of the petition to the Legislature. Does any one know when it was circulated or signed? There may have been debate in the Assembly on the reference of the petition when presented, which might contain interesting facts.

"'*To the Senate and House of Representatives of the Commonwealth of Pennsylvania:* The petition of the subscribers respectfully sheweth, That the State of Pennsylvania has been greatly benefited by the results of the experiments lately so successfully made to manufacture iron with anthracite coal. They conceive that these results are mainly to be attributed to the exertion of William Lyman, of Schuylkill County, who, at his own risk and expense, put into successful operation in this country the first anthracite blast-furnace (on a practical scale), the origin, therefore, of all others since built and now projecting; and they, therefore, pray your honorable bodies that an act may be passed conferring on him such privileges as in your wisdom may be deemed expedient; thereby encouraging useful enterprises in future, and affording some compensation for the heavy outlays always necessarily incident to the commencement of every such undertaking.'

"'POTTSVILLE, Oct. 14th, 1840.

"'This is to certify to all whom it may concern, that all contracts or bargains for ore which may be made by the bearer, Mr. Lance, will be confirmed by Messrs. Marshall & Kellogg, proprietors of the anthracite furnace at this place; and all ore purchased by Mr. Lance will be paid for by city acceptance, as shall be agreed on between the parties.—For Marshall & Kellogg. WM. LYMAN.'"

The following article is from the *Pottsville Miners' Journal:*

"This subject has again been broached in a letter wnich we published a few days ago from James Pott, in which he stated that his father, John Pott, was the first to make anthracite iron at his furnace in 1837-38, located in the West Branch Valley. This we know is correct as far as it goes; but in the use of anthracite coal alone he failed in making it in a merchantable quantity, and ceased working until the trial was made at the Pioneer Furnace on the Island in 1839. After the success at the Pioneer Furnace, he did intend to remodel his furnace to use anthracite coal exclusively; but a freshet came and swept away his works, and he moved to Bedford—now Fulton—County. Mr. Geisenheimer made a small quantity of anthracite iron at the Valley Furnace, and took out a patent, but afterwards abandoned it. Small quantities were made on the Lehigh; and we believe that the late Mr. Ridgway succeeded in making a small quantity at the old Pott Furnace near the Island. But, as they were all charcoal furnaces, of course no quantity could be made. Anthracite iron was also made in Wales. But these experiments satisfied Burd Patterson, and other parties deeply interested in coal and iron interests, that iron could be made with anthracite coal; and then he and other parties commenced building the Pioneer Furnace on the Island after the model of the furnace in Wales, which Mr. David Thomas had seen, and who superintended the building of this furnace. They ran out of funds, and the late Nicholas Biddle and others made up a fund of $5000 as a premium, which they offered to any person who would make anthracite iron for commercial use, and run the furnace for a period of six months. Mr. William Lyman then took the furnace, and completed it after the model of the Wales furnace, which Mr. Thomas furnished. When finished, the furnace was blown in by Mr. Benjamin Perry; and it was a success, and the furnace was kept running for the period of six months. The premium, after full investigation, was awarded to Mr. Lyman, at the Mount Carbon House, in 1840, where a supper was given, and it was at this supper that Nicholas Biddle gave the following toast:

"'OLD PENNSYLVANIA—her sons like her soil—rough outside, but solid stuffed within; plenty of coal to warm her friends, and plenty of iron to cool her enemies.'

"The iron trade at that time was so much depressed under the compromise tariff of 1833, reducing the duties down to 20 per cent. in 1840, and the opposition to the use of anthracite iron by the charcoal interests, that Mr. Lyman failed a short time after; then Mr. Marshall, now of Shamokin, ran it afterwards, and he met with the same fate. The furnace was afterwards run by other parties who had but little capital, and they too failed, when it finally fell into the hands of the Atkins Brothers, who took charge of it in 1857 or 1858, and they too became to some extent involved, owing to the dull state of the iron trade under the free-trade system; and if it had not been for the Rebellion occurring in 1861–62, which put up the price of iron, they might have met the same fate; but they succeeded, and added another furnace to the old Pioneer; then tore down and remodeled the Pioneer, and are now erecting a third furnace on the Island on a larger scale than the others. Of the three brothers, our citizen, Mr. Chas. Atkins, is the only survivor. After the success at the Pioneer, other parties, avoiding the defects of the old Pioneer, erected other furnaces on the Lehigh and elsewhere, and anthracite iron was soon made in large quantities, and in 1871, out of 1,914,000 tons of iron produced in the United States, 957,608 tons, a little more than one-half of the supply, was made with anthracite coal. In 1861 the product was 409,229 tons, having more than doubled in ten years.

"These are the facts connected with the first manufacture of anthracite iron for commerce in the United States; and Mr. Lyman, who undertook the furnace, Mr. David Thomas, who superintended its erection, Mr. Benjamin Perry, who blew it in successfully, and the gentlemen who offered the premium of $5000 for its production in commercial quantities, are really entitled to the credit of establishing this branch of business in this country; while the other gentlemen, who had previously made small quantities before it was made in England, are entitled to the credit of demonstrating that it could be made with suitable fixtures; but they all failed in making it in quantities for use."

The concluding letter was published in the *Mauch Chunk Democrat:*

"TRENTON, N. J., May 4th, 1872.

"MR. EDITOR:

"DEAR SIR,—In the *Journal* of March 30th last, you published for me a communication containing some extracts from a work issued during the year 1841 by Prof. Walter R. Johnson, of Philadelphia, entitled 'Notes on the Use of Anthracite in the Manufacture of Iron; with some Remarks on its Evaporative Power.'

"My object in sending you that article was simply to defend my former partners and myself from the detractive remarks made in a letter written by David Thomas, Esq., of Catasauqua, Pa.; he having stated that our furnace at Mauch Chunk *chilled up in about one week after blowing-in,* whereas it, in fact, was not allowed to chill up at any time.

"Since my communication was written, I have read two or three articles from different papers asserting that I was detracting from the credit due Mr. Thomas.

"I have no wish to claim any 'glory' rightfully belonging to Mr. Thomas, or to others. I merely, in defending the firm of B., G. & Co. from Mr. T.'s unjust remark, quoted authentic history published more than thirty years ago, and which has never been contradicted.

"Some of the parties who have been writing in

behalf of Mr. Thomas, but who evidently know little about the smelting of iron ore, speak rather contemptuously of us because we operated with a small furnace.

"In a matter which at that time was looked upon, even by iron-masters, with much uncertainty as to its ultimate success, it would have been very unwise to go to the expense of building a large furnace at a cost of many thousands of dollars, when it was known that if the thing could be accomplished with a *small furnace, it could be done much more easily, and far more profitably, with a large one.*

"We did not enlarge our furnace, as one writer has stated, but simply the hearth, and we blew it out because it was too small to work at profit; and, not having funds with which to construct large works, we returned the property on which the furnace was built to the L. C. & N. Co., from whom it was leased, which was the last we had to do with it.

"A few years afterward I was introduced to a gentleman from Pottsville, who, upon being informed by our friend that I had been connected with the Mauch Chunk furnace, asked if I recollected a committee of the citizens of Pottsville visiting us one night. I answered in the affirmative, and asked him what conclusion they arrived at. He replied, 'We watched you all night long, and returned home with the full conclusion that it was a perfect success.'

"Within the past week or two I have seen one or two articles from the pen of Mr. James Pott, of Harrisburg, who claims for his father, Mr. John Pott, the credit of having been the first in this country to smelt iron ore with anthracite. He dates his first success so far back as 1836 and '37. A more unpresuming and candid letter than that of Mr. Pott I have never read; and if we are to look outside of published history for the one who was first successful, I should say that without a doubt (so far as I can learn) Mr. John Pott, of the Manheim furnace, was the man.

"Very respectfully yours,

"F. C. LOWTHROP."

We add an article from the *Mauch Chunk Coal Gazette* of May 25th, 1872:

"Mr. James Cornelison, formerly a blacksmith residing here, was in town on Monday last, and was 'interviewed' concerning his knowledge of the first experiments in the manufacture of anthracite iron. He was employed in the establishment of the Lehigh Coal and Navigation Company, whose works were upon the site of the present foundry of J. H. Salkeld & Co., and distinctly remembers the building about the year 1823 or 1824 of a stack some 15 or 20 feet high, for the purpose of smelting the iron ore with anthracite coal. This experiment was, at the time, so far successful, that Mr. Cornelison states several 'pigs' were actually made with cold-air blast. Messrs. Josiah White and Erskine Hazard were concerned in the building of the stack, in whose operations much interest was taken. This statement, coming from a gentleman in every way reliable, makes good the assertion in Johnson's 'Notes on Anthracite Iron,' that the first known experiment in this important direction was made in Mauch Chunk."

APPENDIX C.

In this age of railroads, it seems almost incredible that there should have been much difficulty in persuading the community of their feasibility and superiority; and we are very apt to overlook the signal benefits conferred upon mankind by those who had the faith and courage to advocate them amid such general opposition. Among such benefactors in America, no one deserves a higher rank than Colonel John Stevens, of Hoboken, New Jersey, the father of two sons, Robert L. and Edwin A., whose achievements in mechanics and science were of a like eminent character.

In 1812, Colonel Stevens published a pamphlet (very rare now, even in its reprint of 1852), entitled, "Documents tending to prove the Superior Advantages of Railways and Steam Carriages over Canal Navigation." At that time, not a locomotive existed in the world, and the only railroads were the few and short tramways in use mostly at the coal mines in England. A plan had been suggested of bringing the waters of Lake Erie by a canal, on an inclined plane of three hundred miles in length, to communicate with the Hudson River. This proposition, in those early days, was looked upon as being very bold and grand. But Stevens, in a communication addressed to the Commissioners appointed by the Legislature to explore the route for this projected inland navigation, submitted a scheme of what he deemed a better way of accomplishing this same object.

"Let a railway of timber be formed," he writes,

"by the nearest practicable route between Lake Erie and Albany. The angle of elevation in no part to exceed one degree, or such an elevation, whatever it may be, as will admit of wheel-carriages to remain stationary when no power is exerted to impel them forward. This railway, throughout its course, to be supported on pillars raised from three to five or six feet from the surface of the ground. The carriage-wheels of cast-iron, the rims flat, with projecting flanges to fit on the surface of the railways. The moving-power to be a steam-engine, nearly similar in construction to that on board the Juliana, a ferry-boat plying between this city and Hoboken."*

He proceeds to mention the advantages to result from adopting his plan, arguing in its favor because of its cheapness; its saving of time in construction; its freedom from decay, from interruption in storms, and from casualties; its economy in the expense of transportation. As to the speed that might be attained, he estimates, "after every possible reduction for exaggeration," that it might reach *four miles an hour.*

From the general incredulity at first manifested in the likelihood of propelling boats by steam, he is prepared for tardiness in accepting his theories concerning the propulsion by steam of cars, although he urged that there was no more difficulty in the one case than in the other. After going into minute and scientific calcula-

---

* The *Juliana* was built by Colonel Stevens in 1811, her engine being of the model patented by himself. The steam was used expansively,—cut off in the main valves. She was the first boat to navigate the Sound, as his *Phœnix* was the first, in 1808, to navigate the ocean between Sandy Hook and the Delaware.

tions to substantiate his theories, he adds, "Should these railways be so subject to wear as that the frequency of their renewal becomes inconvenient and expensive, resource could be had at any time to cast or plated iron railways, which, without any further expense or trouble, could be fastened on the top of the wooden railways."

In the following extract from a letter of Chancellor Robert R. Livingston, we have a sample of the objections urged to this scheme even by learned and thoughtful men :

"I have read your very ingenious propositions as to the railway communication. I fear, however, on mature reflection, that they will be liable to serious objections, and ultimately more expensive than a canal. They must be double, so as to prevent the danger of two such heavy bodies meeting. *The walls on which they are placed must be at least four feet below the surface, and three above, and must be clamped with iron; and even then would hardly sustain so heavy a weight as you propose moving at the rate of four miles an hour on wheels.* As to wood, it would not last a week; they must be covered with iron, and that, too, very thick and strong. *The means of stopping these heavy carriages without a great shock, and of preventing them from running upon each other, would be very difficult. In case of accidental stops, or the necessary stops to take wood and water, etc., many accidents would happen. The carriage of condensing-water would be very troublesome.* Upon the whole, I fear the expense would be much greater than that of canals, *without being so convenient.*"*

* Similar views seem to have been entertained by the Managers of the Lehigh Coal and Navigation Company, who, in their report for the

To this letter of his distinguished brother-in-law, Colonel Stevens replies at length, detailing the comparative cost of constructing railroad and canal, and showing how much would be saved in building the former. So, too, he shows how much more convenient it would be than the latter. And in communications to Gouverneur Morris and De Witt Clinton, he still further argues his cause, with a sagacity simply surprising in days so remote from the employment of railways. He modestly asks for the sum of three thousand dollars, with which to make experiments, predicting that the practical benefits to be derived from them by the country at large would far outweigh the value of this sum.

His communications were referred to a committee, who, through Gouverneur Morris, reported adversely to the project. Their answer is evidently prepared with great care, and is mainly based upon supposed scientific principles. They give the preference, in drawing a weight, to horses, because of their having a more sufficient hold upon the earth. The rims of the engine-wheels, it was thought, would by their friction impede the progressive motion. Great danger was apprehended from the warping of logs by change of weather. Similar difficulty was anticipated from the wheel-rims and railway not fitting exactly. After an elaborate argument, they conclude that it is not probable that a way could be made of sufficient strength to warrant

---

year 1841, say of the railroad they were then building to connect their canal with the North Branch Canal, that "it has already excited much attention, and will unquestionably form *a feeder of great value to our canal.*"

such speed as the rate of four miles per hour, "which," say the committee, "*is nearly two yards in a second.*"

In answer to this report, Colonel Stevens writes, that the objections therein urged "have only served to establish more firmly in my mind the very favorable sentiments I entertain respecting the practical utility of the proposed railways." Want of space forbids our giving here the various arguments by which he combated these objections. Suffice it to say, that they do him great credit even in this period of advanced knowledge upon the whole subject, and almost startle us with the accuracy of their predictions. In alluding to the question of velocity, he says,—be it remembered, in 1812,—that, while it may not in practice be convenient to exceed twenty or thirty miles per hour, he would not be surprised at seeing steam-carriages propelled at the rate of forty or fifty miles, and he thinks of nothing to hinder them from moving at the rate of one hundred miles per hour.

It is a matter of congratulation that he had the satisfaction of living to see his predictions verified, and of himself riding upon a railway (the Camden and Amboy), constructed under the supervision of his son, at the rate of fifty miles an hour.

APPENDIX D.

GLEN ONOKO.

This beautiful glen is situated two miles above Mauch Chunk, and has lately been made so convenient of access that it is now deservedly attracting large numbers of visitors throughout the year.

It is a striking freak of nature, and reveals pictures of grandeur and magnificence not often excelled. Its course is westerly, and the total ascent over 900 feet. It forms the channel for a pure and limpid stream which follows its eccentric course over innumerable cascades and rapids, and through grottoes and ravines, until it empties, near what is known as the Turnhole Bridge, into the Lehigh, the river at this point making, perhaps, the sharpest turn visible along its entire length.

At the outset, we come upon the

ENTRANCE CASCADE AND POOL,

which, with their bright ripples and foam, and with the huge banks of rhododendron (when in bloom presenting a gorgeous appearance) surrounding them, give us at once a most favorable impression of the treasures embraced within the gorge.

For some distance the railroad company have laid wooden pipes for the supply of the water-tank near the depot.

Proceeding a few feet, we arrive at a neat rustic bridge, from which we have a full view of

CHAMELEON FALLS.

(50 FEET HIGH.) Page 176.

CRYSTAL CASCADE,

whose transparent waters, gurgling over the rocks and glistening in the sunlight, establish their just claim to the name by which they are distinguished. Looking to our back, down the rocky and leafy arcade, we obtain a very pretty sketch of the river and the bridges crossing the Lehigh, including the covered entrance into the tunnel of the Lehigh and Susquehanna Division of the N. J. Central Railroad.

Just above, on our left, we come to the cleft

PULPIT ROCKS,

some twenty feet high, standing as stately ushers into the romantic scenery awaiting us. They are covered with delicate moss and ferns, and from their top may be had a most artistic view of the

MOSSY CASCADE,

which comes dashing over the moss-covered rocks into the pellucid pools below, singing a cheerful welcome to the weary traveler, who, in this sylvan retreat, cannot but be invigorated by the healthy and refreshing air with which he is constantly surrounded.

We next reach the

LAUREL CASCADE,

flowing swiftly by immense growths of laurel, interspersed here and there with the graceful branches of the bright yew tree. Through the majestic hemlocks we are delighted with a distant glimpse of Chameleon Falls.

We have now arrived at what has been termed

THE HEART OF THE GLEN,

from the dark and impenetrable masses of foliage on every side, and from the lively character of the scenes around us. Whichever way we look, we are greeted with wild and weird prospects well calculated to elicit our wonderment and awe.

Here are situated the

STAIRWAY CASCADES,

a series of minor rapids, overleaping one another along a continuous distance of at least 200 feet, shining resplendently amid the different hues and tints of the disordered and water-carved rocks over which they flow so musically.

At this point there has been thrown across the stream an artistic bridge leading up by an ingeniously contrived stairway (made from a gigantic hemlock) to a slight eminence, whence we obtain what is deemed by many to be

THE FINEST VIEW IN THE GLEN.

It includes not only the Chameleon Falls, immediately in front of us, but also the Onoko Falls, some distance beyond, and this double vista is rich with a diversity of beauty not easy to describe. The cliffs about us rising to a towering height, the rhododendron encircling us, the clouds rolling along over the hill-tops, the shadows chasing each other through the trees and over the rocks, the veils of mist floating in the distance, and the steady flow of the silvery waterfalls,—all enchant us, and we pronounce the trip already a grand success.

A look down the glen also from this same point is

ONOKO FALLS.
(90 FEET HIGH.)

Page 179.

sure to elicit enthusiastic admiration of its manifold features of sublimity.

A short walk on either side of the stream brings us in full view of the

Chameleon Falls.

They are so called from the variety of colors so often noticeable in the spray and foam. They are about 50 feet high, and with a full stream present a most beautiful appearance. The water falls into a half-square basin, with a log leaning picturesquely against it. On either side, the dense and variegated foliage makes a charming contrast to the sombre walls of native rock rising so majestically.

By an attractive route we are next conducted to

Onoko Falls,

which are the highest in the glen, and by many esteemed the handsomest. Their height is 90 feet, and they will certainly receive the encomium of all lovers of natural beauty. The shelving, overhanging rocks on either side rise above us most grandly, and covered as they are with moss and fern, a tree now and then jutting from out their apparently sterile embrace, they form a fitting embellishment to the dashing and sparkling waters which have been for centuries seeking through their fissures an outlet from their mountain source.

If we go behind the falls, we can obtain a sight of them which will (especially when the sun is shining) amply repay us for the slight moistening which we may thereby run the risk of receiving.

To any one suffering from the summer's heat a sojourn in the vicinity of these falls may be confidently recommended. The atmosphere is always most cool and refreshing. Snow has been found here as late as the 20th of May. Nor is it only attractive in the summer season, but a visit to them

In the Winter

is most interesting. The appearance of the falls and of the adjoining rocks for 300 feet in circumference, all encased in snow, with all manner of icy stalactites and stalagmites depending and ascending everywhere, is truly magnificent.

After descending the height already noted, the water falls over a ledge of rocks immediately under it, and forms the

Rainbow Cascade,

so called from the fact of rainbows being often visible here in all their gorgeous hues, giving a completeness to the scenery which makes it one of the most delightful spots in the glen.

A few winters ago, as a gentleman from Mauch Chunk was making the tour of the glen, he discovered at the foot of these falls the dead body of a deer which had, no doubt, leaped from their summit to escape the hunter's hounds.

On ascending the path leading from this point we soon come to what has been aptly styled

The Fat Man's Misery,

being a narrow passage through two erect birch trees which will be found rather uncomfortable for any one given to corpulency.

A little farther on there runs the old

WARRIOR PATH,

being the war-trail used, it may be for centuries, by the Indians in passing from the Susquehanna to the Delaware. It was also traversed by General Sullivan and his brave army after the bloody Wyoming massacre in the year 1778, and subsequently by the lumberman in plying his trade, whence it was known as the Raftsman's Path.

We are soon at the head of Onoko Falls, which we must cross to gain the magnificent view from Sunrise Point. It is said that a former resident of this valley (now deceased) once made here a narrow escape from death. He had been belated in the woods, and in following the bed of the stream on his way out he came of a sudden to the summit of the falls. He was proceeding cautiously and was stopped on the edge of the precipice by the dim sight of the trees below. Another step would have landed him inanimate where the poor deer was found.

The student of geology will find much to interest him in the study of the various formations of rock seen along our route, and will be amused, while he rests himself on the conveniently-located seats, at some grotesque appearances which are thus oftentimes presented. In one place near the Onoko Falls there is an almost perfect representation of a camel crouching beneath a heavy burden, and the imagination can easily discern other animals and figures.

Having crossed the head of Onoko Falls to the left, we are brought to

SUNRISE POINT,

from which, looking eastward, there is spread out before the eye a panorama of rare and enchanting beauty. In quick succession we see the Lehigh River, East Mauch Chunk, and Mount Pisgah, and then, stretching still farther southward, the Lehigh Water Gap, all laid out most picturesquely, forming a landscape upon which we willingly pause to feast ourselves. We begin now to realize how high we have traveled, and how full of interest is every turn in our route, furnishing ample material for the artist's pencil or the poet's pen.

We next climb the

RUSTIC STAIRWAY,

and find ourselves rather abruptly at the

TERRACE FALLS,

the water descending impetuously over a ledge of rocks which almost seem as though they had been terraced with the precision and skill of the artisan.

Another short walk brings us to the

CAVE FALLS.

These derive their name from the cave in their immediate rear, into which quite a large party can enter. Looking from behind the falls, the perspective is singularly handsome and romantic. Around us we will find the remnants of lists of visitors' names who have ventured here to enjoy the novel scene, while upon the rocks may be seen the more enduring record of such tourists as have come provided with paint and brush.

For several hundred feet we are now conducted by a

wild and fantastic path along beds of the sweet trailing arbutus, and by the side of a ceaseless round of cascades and torrents, to the summit of the mountain, and to

THE HUNTER'S ROCK-CABIN,

built many years ago, and much frequented over-night by sportsmen, who, sheltered by hemlock boughs and warmed by their wood-fires, slept soundly enough, disturbed only by their vivid dreams of the exciting scenes of their day's chase and travel.

This will be a convenient spot for us to rest a while and eat our lunch, which in every instance will need to be generously provided. Here, too, we will entertain each other by our enthusiastic admiration of the grand and beautiful sights which our entire passage through the glen has afforded us, and lift at least a silent tribute of praise to the Divine Architect of the universe, Whose handiwork is everywhere so manifest. After resting and lunching, the traveler should on no account fail to cross the stream here and proceed by the path recently made, over what has been called "The Lava Beds," to

PACKER'S POINT,

named in honor of Hon. Asa Packer, President of the Lehigh Valley Railroad Company. It is less than a quarter of a mile, perhaps, from the cabin, and were it much farther even, we all should feel more than rewarded for our walk by the really superb view which may be here so thoroughly enjoyed. From the lookout erected on the rocks we can see for miles up and down the Lehigh, to the bottom of the giddy heights, along the sharp curves, over bridges and less lofty hills, with a full view of East Mauch Chunk, and through the Lehigh Gap of the mountains beyond.

Around us nature is undisturbed. Beneath us, in the railroads and canals, we see how she has been overcome and made subservient to man's wants and pleasures. Beyond we are confronted with his settlements, and on the very tops of the distant mountains we recognize the results of his toil in the green and fertile fields adorning them. The eye thus takes in at a glance a diminutive picture of the world at large, and conveys to the soul fresh inspiration for the stern realities of our every-day life. No one can dwell upon such scenery as is here afforded without receiving a stimulus of the most wholesome character, and again we urge the tourist not to return from the glen without enjoying it.

THE SAND-SPRINGS AND JAMES RUN.

Between one and two miles from the summit of the mountain the tourist may have an additional treat which will abundantly compensate him for any fatigue which he may undergo. We refer first to

The Sand-Springs.

These natural curiosities (at the head of James Run) consist of several large and small springs of various depths, which are continually boiling and bubbling, throwing the water and sand to a height of a foot or more, sometimes beneath the surface of the water and sometimes above it. They are well deserving a visit, and an experienced angler may return with a mess of speckled trout, with which he may regale himself as he recalls the pleasures of his trip.

A short distance below the springs we reach

JAMES RUN,

which is one of the most romantic streams to be found in the State. It contains a large body of water, which flows most charmingly through deep ravines and over huge masses of handsome rocks, forming an endless series of very lovely waterfalls and cascades, some of which are of considerable height and length. The whole course of the stream is one of real grandeur and beauty, displaying at every turn something fresh to admire, and furnishing many most attractive pictures, over which one may delight himself for hours. To one fond of trouting this stream offers an incentive which will make him only too anxious to repeat his trip.

APPENDIX E.

SAYRE.

At this station (named in honor of Mr. Robert H. Sayre, President of the P. & N. Y. C. & R. R. Company) connection is made with the Southern Central R. R. for Auburn and Syracuse on the N. Y. Central R. R., and Fair Haven and Oswego on Lake Ontario, and with the Ithaca & Athens R. R. for Ithaca, the seat of Cornell University, at the head of Cayuga Lake. The P. & N. Y. C. & R. R. Co. have about 60 acres of land at this point, and have built a handsome brick round-house with stalls for 15 engines. Space has also been reserved for the erection of machine-shops and other buildings when required. Car-shops will probably be put up during the present year.

A planing-mill has just been erected near the depot, and a short distance above, the Cayuta Wheel Foundry Company have built substantial works for the manufacture of car-wheels, with a present capacity of about 50 pairs per day. The land in the vicinity of the depot has been laid out in building lots, streets have been opened, several houses have been erected, and other improvements are in contemplation which will afford a nucleus for a thriving settlement.

www.ingramcontent.com/pod-product-compliance
Lightning Source LLC
LaVergne TN
LVHW011214110826
845150LV00006B/1428

* 9 7 8 1 4 2 5 5 1 7 0 1 4 *